Cambridge Practice Tests for PET 1

TEACHER'S BOOK

*Louise Hashemi and
Barbara Thomas*

CAMBRIDGE
UNIVERSITY

PUBLISHED BY THE PRESS SYNDICATE OF THE UNIVERSITY OF CAMBRIDGE
The Pitt Building, Trumpington Street, Cambridge, United Kingdom

CAMBRIDGE UNIVERSITY PRESS
The Edinburgh Building, Cambridge CB2 2RU, UK
40 West 20th Street, New York, NY 10011–4211, USA
10 Stamford Road, Oakleigh, VIC 3166, Australia
Ruiz de Alarcón 13, 28014 Madrid, Spain
Dock House, The Waterfront, Cape Town 8001, South Africa

http://www.cambridge.org

First published 1996
Fourth printing 2000

Printed in the United Kingdom at the University Press, Cambridge

ISBN 0 521 49938 0 Student's Book
ISBN 0 521 49939 9 Teacher's Book
ISBN 0 521 49940 2 Set of 2 cassettes

Contents

Thanks

The authors would like to thank everyone at CUP for their help and support during the production of this book. We are also grateful to the subject officers at UCLES who have patiently answered our queries.

The authors and publishers would like to thank the following teachers and their students for piloting the material for *Cambridge Practice Tests for PET 1*: Caroline Atkinson, English Language Centre, Liverpool; Mary G. Boyd, The British Council, Bologna; Mary de Freitas, Madrid; Janet Golding, Anglo World, Bournemouth; Alec Ling, Bouzille; C. McDade, Dewsbury College, Dewsbury; Katy Thorne, Teikyo University of Japan, Durham.

Introduction

The Preliminary English Test – PET – was introduced by the University of Cambridge Local Examinations Syndicate (UCLES) in the late 1970s in response to a demand for an examination at a level lower than the First Certificate in English. It was substantially revised in 1988/9. OMR (Optical Mark Reader) answer sheets were introduced in 1994 for all parts of the examination (see page 44), which involved some changes to questions which had previously been marked in other ways. In 1996 there were further minor changes to some questions. This set of Practice Tests takes all the changes into account.

The level of the PET

Candidates who pass the PET are expected to be at the Council of Europe Threshold Level as defined by van Ek and Trim in 1990, which requires approximately 350 hours of dedicated study. The language level of the PET is considered by UCLES to be approximately two-thirds of the way towards that of the First Certificate in English. Candidates who pass the PET should be able to communicate satisfactorily in a range of everyday situations with both native and non-native speakers of English.

The structure of the PET

The examination consists of Paper 1 (Reading and Writing), Paper 2 (Listening) and the Speaking test.

Paper 1	1 hour 30 mins	Reading	5 parts	35 marks weighted to 25
		Writing	3 parts	25 marks
Paper 2	30 mins + 12 mins transfer time	Listening	4 parts	25 marks
Speaking	Individual: 8 mins approx. Pair: 10 mins approx.		4 parts	25 marks

Using these Practice Tests

The five tests in this book mirror the actual PET exam and give students practice in the skills needed to answer the questions. The first test is different from the others because, for each part, students are given information about the questions and advice on answering them. They are not given the answers, however, so it can still be used as a test if required, or alternatively, as a classroom or homework learning exercise.

Disabled candidates and special needs

Students who need special help or consideration, for example, the blind, deaf or otherwise physically disadvantaged, should contact UCLES at the address given, for information about the ways in which they can be helped to take the examination. UCLES will provide suitably modified papers, and arrangements can be made for help at the time of the examination. Students with learning difficulties, for example dyslexia, may receive special consideration if they can provide suitable documentation. Teachers should also be aware that it might be worth informing UCLES if students have had serious personal problems (such as bereavement) around the time of the exam.

Taking the PET

The PET can be taken six times a year. Paper 1 (Reading and Writing) is immediately followed by Paper 2 (Listening) and they take place on one morning. Further administrative details and a list of examination centres is available from UCLES.

For more information about all UCLES exams, write to:
UCLES
1 Hills Road
Cambridge
CB1 2EU
England

A guide to the papers

Reading

The Reading section consists of five parts, making a total of 35 questions.

Part	Text	Questions	Question no.
Part 1	5 signs	5 multiple choice questions, each with 4 options	1–5
Part 2	8 related texts	5 descriptions of people to be matched to the texts	6–10
Part 3	Information text	10 true/false questions	11–20
Part 4	Text with opinion or attitude	5 multiple choice questions, each with 4 options	21–25
Part 5	Cloze text (one word per gap)	10 multiple choice questions, each with 4 options	26–35

The Reading part of the PET exam requires candidates to use different reading strategies so it is important that students have practice in a wide range of reading activities. They should get used to reading for detail, reading for the main idea and scanning for specific information. The more exposure they have to authentic reading materials in English the better, e.g. newspaper and magazine articles, reviews, advertisements, brochures and leaflets, instructions, etc. It is important, however, that they do not become discouraged when they realise they cannot understand everything – remind them that they do not take in everything they read even in their own language. Simplified readers are very useful at this level and will help students improve their vocabulary and reading speed. In some areas of the world, there may be no authentic English publications available so students should read as much as possible in publications for learners of English.

Part 1

Candidates are presented with five signs or notices. They are based on authentic signs that a candidate may come across in public places in an English-speaking environment. Each sign is accompanied by a four-option multiple choice question, only one of the options conveying the exact meaning of the sign. There is a standard example showing candidates what to do.

Preparing students
- If students are studying in an English-speaking country, encourage them to note down signs in English which they come across and discuss them in class. If you do not have access to signs, try translating some signs in your own

language which have international significance. A lot of signs are common to all countries so this could be good practice for the kinds of signs which may appear in the exam, although there are obviously some which are too difficult for students with PET level of competence in English.

- Explain that unimportant words like articles and pronouns are often missing in signs.
- Students can try to guess where the signs might have appeared as this will help them with the context.
- Make sure students realise that the correct multiple choice option must have *exactly* the same meaning as the main message of the sign, although some of the other options may be close.

Part 2

Candidates are presented with five short descriptions of individuals or groups of people which have to be matched with eight short descriptions or advertisements on a related theme, e.g. holidays, activities, books, films, TV programmes, etc. Only one of the eight descriptions suits each individual/group exactly. Three of the descriptions are not needed.

Preparing students
- Remind students that only one description matches each person and some of the other descriptions may fit in some ways but not all. They should go back and check when they have finished to make sure they haven't missed something.
- If possible, give students practice in this kind of matching task. They could try to find a book in the school library which matches the interests of a fellow student. If you have access to catalogues in English, they could try to find presents to suit particular people, or holidays from holiday brochures.

Part 3

Candidates read a fairly long text (about 400 words), such as an advertisement, an extract from a brochure, an information sheet or a public notice, and then answer ten true/false questions about it. The questions are in the same order as the information in the text.

Preparing students
- Advise students to read the questions and then to look through the text to get a general idea of what it is about. Remind them that they do not need to understand every word as there will not be a question on every part of the text.
- When they have understood the gist of the text, they should go back to the first question, find the part of the text which it refers to and decide whether it is true or false, according to the information given. A highlighter pen may be useful.
- Give students practice in scanning. Give them a text and ask them to find the answers to a few questions so that they learn to disregard material which is not necessary to the task.
- If some candidates find this kind of reading exercise difficult because they

want to understand every word, get them to do the same kind of exercise in their own language to demonstrate the skill required. They will probably be surprised that in their own language they do not read and take in every word when looking for specific information.

Part 4

Candidates read a text such as a review, an advertisement or a letter, which conveys an attitude or opinion as well as information. They answer five multiple choice questions about the text to show that they have understood the purpose of the text, the attitude or opinion of the writer, the global meaning and the detailed meaning.

Preparing students

- Give students practice in answering questions about the source of texts and the writer's purpose. They need to learn to look for clues which point to the source and to recognise different styles and register at the most basic level. One way of starting this work with students is to provide sentences from a range of sources such as personal letters, advertisements, public information leaflets, etc. Invite the class to guess where you found them. This can be a team game, with points scored both for good guesses and correct identification of 'clues'.
- Tell students that some of the questions test their understanding of the whole text and some test their understanding of detail. On the first reading, they should try to understand the general meaning of the text.
- The last question which tests global meaning may be text or pictures. They need to look at this question carefully, taking all aspects of the text into consideration, before they answer.
- Remind candidates about there being only one correct answer for each multiple choice question, even though some options look close.

Part 5

This is a Cloze test with ten single-word gaps, plus an example. For each gap, there are four options, only one of which is correct in the context. The text is either factual or narrative. The questions test both lexical and structural knowledge.

Preparing students

- When answering this question, students should first read the text through and get an idea of the general meaning before they try to fill the gaps.
- Students should then look at the gaps, reading around them (both before *and after*) to decide what kind of word fits, e.g. noun, adjective, etc.
- In order to choose the correct option for the gap, students can try fitting each one into the gap in turn and reading the whole sentence to see if it makes sense.
- Make some Cloze tests yourself by deleting words from texts which the students are already familiar with or texts which the students have written themselves. Students can practise the skills of deducing meaning from context and reading words in groups. For this, they just need the gapped text and can

provide the missing words themselves. In the exam, they are also given the support of the multiple choice questions. Later on, you may wish to make Cloze tests from texts which the students have not seen before and then, possibly, make up your own multiple choice questions.

Writing

The Writing section consists of three parts, carrying a total of 25 marks.

Part	Task	Questions	Question no.
Part 1	Sentence transformations	5 questions plus an example	1–5
Part 2	Form	10 gaps on form	6–15
Part 3	Letter	Continuous prose of about 100 words	16

Students at this level are making the transition from writing sentences to writing longer pieces of prose. The first two tasks in the PET exam are very controlled and test writing at the word, phrase and sentence level. The third task is an extended piece of writing and students need practice in structuring something longer than a few sentences. They may like to start writing to penfriends in English-speaking countries or they could keep a diary in English. At first, they need to plan what they are going to say and get their ideas down without worrying too much about mistakes. Once they have mastered the idea of writing 100 words of continuous prose, they can start looking more carefully at the accuracy of their language.

Part 1

Candidates are asked to rewrite a sentence using a different structural pattern but retaining the same meaning. They are given the beginning of the sentence which they have to finish. The sentences are related to a theme and there is an example at the beginning to show candidates what to do. There may be more than one correct answer in each case.

Preparing students
- This task tests the students' grammar. Some students find it helpful to practise identifying the *type* of structural transformation needed (e.g. passive to active voice or direct to reported speech) before attempting to rewrite the sentence. It is a good idea to incorporate exercises of this sort when practising new structures in class.
- Remind students that the new sentence must have exactly the same meaning as the original one. Get them to go back and check that this is the case when they have finished each transformation. They may have missed out a word or two and thus changed the meaning.
- If students find the concept of transformations problematic, the following exercise may help. Choose some sentences which the students know well (e.g.

from their own work). Write transformed versions and give these to the students, with the first word or two of the original sentences. The students, with help if necessary, will eventually produce their own original sentences. This exercise can later be developed into a game in which groups produce exercises for each other.

Part 2

Candidates are presented with a form and are required to fill in specific information about themselves by writing words, numbers and short phrases in the ten gaps.

Preparing students
* Some of the questions appear on every test so students can practise these and other questions which are likely to come up.
* Remind them that you do not need to write sentences on a form – one or two words is usually enough. However, they should imagine that this is a real form so the information supplied should be adequate, e.g. the address should be complete.

Part 3

Candidates are asked to write a letter of about 100 words. They are given the context and the first sentence. They are expected to be able to use a range of structures and vocabulary and to organise their thoughts coherently in order to complete the task.

Preparing students
* Get students to practise writing about 100 words. Once they know what 100 words of their own writing looks like, they will have a good idea when they have written the required amount without having to count every word.
* In the exam, students are not required to set out the address although the task must be written in the style of a letter.
* Make sure students learn to answer the question. Half the marks are given for completing the task so, even if they write in perfect English, they will not get a good mark if they have not answered the question.
* If students complain that they can't think what to write, have class or group 'brain-storming' sessions, put the results on the board and show the students how to choose and order ideas before beginning to write.
* Some students have a lot of difficulty in controlling their language at the same time as using their imagination. It is never too early to start learning the following discipline:
  – define your task
  – note down your ideas
  – put them in order
  – write
  – check

Listening

The Listening Paper consists of four parts, making a total of 25 questions.

Part	Text	Questions	Question no.
Part 1	7 short dialogues or monologues	7 multiple choice questions (pictorial), each with 4 options	1–7
Part 2	Monologue	6 multiple choice questions, each with 4 options	8–13
Part 3	Monologue or prompted monologue	6 gap-filling questions	14–19
Part 4	Dialogue	6 true/false questions	20–25

The amount of practice students get in hearing spoken English will depend where they are studying. Wherever they are, they should try to speak English as much as possible, whether to English-speaking friends or their own classmates. In some countries, English-language programmes may be broadcast on the radio. Although some of these may be difficult for students at PET level, they should be able to understand the gist of what is being said and it will get them used to hearing English spoken in a range of situations. For details of British overseas broadcasts, write to The BBC, Bush House, PO Box 76, The Strand, London WC2 4PH. Some students may enjoy watching films in English on video or listening to songs in English on cassette. Many cassettes and CDs have the words with them.

Part 1

Candidates hear seven short recordings of a few sentences each. Each one is played twice. They are unrelated and may be dialogues or monologues. For each one, candidates are asked a focus question (on the tape and on the question paper) and, in order to answer, they have to choose between four pictures, only one of which sums up what they have heard and answers the focus question.

Preparing students
• This task is easier for students who have had plenty of practice in using and hearing English for everyday purposes. Those students who have only been exposed to 'classroom' English will have more difficulty 'tuning in' quickly, especially if situations are usually set up in their own language. Try to ensure that, as far as possible, only English is used in the language classroom, even for administrative purposes.
• Give students practice in listening to small snatches of English and understanding the main idea of what is being said.
• As a classroom activity, students can look at the pictures before they listen. They can think of some of the words needed in English to describe them and examine them for differences so they will have an idea of what to listen for on the tape. In the exam, they won't have much time to do this but it is still useful for them to have a quick look at the pictures before listening.

- The focus question can give an idea of what is going to come on the tape, e.g. it is about a journey.
- Remind students that only one picture is the correct answer, even though aspects of the others may be mentioned.

Part 2

Candidates listen to a fairly long (about 400 words) semi-formal monologue, such as a radio report, a museum tour or a recorded message. They hear it twice and then answer six multiple choice questions, each with four options, which test detailed understanding.

Preparing students

- It is useful if students can look at the questions before they start to listen. They probably won't have time to look at the options but they can at least have an idea of what they need to listen for.
- A particular word in the question, e.g. a proper name, may help students to locate the part of the recording which has the answer.
- Students need to learn to pick out specific points of information from what they hear and distinguish between main and secondary points.
- Students should try to mark their answers on the first listening and then check them on the second. It is easy to make a mistake – a word or phrase may be mentioned, but not actually be the answer to the question. It is worth students checking everything the second time, even if they were certain of the answer the first time they heard it.
- If students find these longer pieces daunting, it may help to compose one or two similar listening exercises, but containing plenty of familiar references, for instance to events and locations known to the students, which can act as markers. From there, it should be easier for the students to progress to similar exercises without familiar references.

Part 3

Candidates hear a monologue, e.g. information about a public place, special arrangements for a group outing, or a prompted monologue (one side of a conversation). It is played twice. From what they hear, they extract the information necessary to complete a form or a note, etc. There are six gaps and each requires one, two or three words to be filled in.

Preparing students

- A lot of what students hear in this task is redundant in terms of answering the questions. It is therefore important that they have a quick look at the questions before listening.
- The first time they listen they should try to get a general understanding and have a go at answering the questions.
- Some students may be worried at not understanding everything they hear. Reassure them that they only need to understand parts of the recording in detail in order to be able to answer the questions.
- If they are not sure how to spell a word, they should write what they think as they will not be penalised for minor spelling mistakes.

Part 4

Candidates hear a dialogue in which two people express opinions and feelings as well as exchanging information and arriving at an outcome. It is played twice. Candidates answer six true/false questions about what they have heard.

Preparing students

- Students should look at the questions before they listen to get an idea of the subject matter.
- While they are listening, they should try to understand how the speakers *feel* about what they are saying as some of the questions will test this.
- Students should read the questions very carefully as, in order to be true, they must have the same meaning as what is said on the recording. The question may say someone *has had* a holiday, whereas the tape says they *are going to have* a holiday, so careful listening and reading are required.
- Oral practice can be closely tied to these questions. Production and recognition of different intonation patterns will be particularly helpful.

Speaking

In the PET, importance is attached to the balance of linguistic skills, with the Speaking test carrying 25 per cent of the final marks. It is important, therefore, that oral work should be given as much time as possible. It is also important to distinguish clearly between *examination practice*, in which students learn what to expect and how to perform at their best under interview conditions, and *preparation*, in which students acquire and practise oral skills, through a variety of classroom materials and activities. These skills will be needed for the purposes of general communication as well as for the examination.

Teachers are advised to study the following notes on the conduct of the Speaking test in conjunction with the frameworks for the Speaking test (see page 14) in order that they may be able to familiarise their students with the structure and procedure of the test. Ideally, each candidate should be given at least one 'mock' Speaking test under examination conditions.

Conduct of the Speaking test

The Speaking test consists of a conversation with an examiner which candidates may take individually or in a pair.* The individual test lasts about eight minutes, the pair about ten. The pair format is generally considered to be preferable, and is recommended in most cases by UCLES as offering a more supportive environment for the candidates, thus enabling them to show their spoken English to best advantage.

The examiner sits at a table, probably arranged at an angle to where the candidate(s) will sit. He or she has the marksheets, and will write on them during the exam. These are not shown to the candidate(s) at any time.

* Another examiner, who does not join in the conversation, will also be present during the Speaking test. He or she is the assessor. Naturally, in practice situations, teachers will normally conduct tests alone but students should be prepared for the presence of the assessor in the actual exam (see picture on page 37 of the Student's Book).

The Speaking test consists of four parts. The four parts are not linked thematically, except that Part 4 follows on from the visual material provided in Part 3. The examiner will not announce the beginning or end of each part but will probably say 'Thank you' at the end, and then go on to say what is to be done next.

The examiner will speak at a normal, but fairly slow, pace. If the candidate is nervous, or does not understand instructions, the examiner will repeat these even more slowly. The examiner may do more talking than in higher level oral examinations, in order to give plenty of support to the candidates, especially with individual candidates and in Parts 1 and 4.

Candidates can expect the examiner to be patient and friendly, but the examiner will not give the candidate any information about how well he or she has done. The examiner will not use expressions such as 'Good' or 'Fine', which candidates might interpret as a comment, nor will any errors be corrected or commented upon. Each Speaking test has a framework of questions and remarks. At some points the examiner may simply pause after he or she has made a remark, to give the candidate an opportunity to initiate a part of the conversation. This is in order to try to avoid the traditional atmosphere of interrogation in oral examinations. The pause will not be allowed to go on too long if the candidate says nothing. The examiner will stick to the framework as much as possible, but will be flexible in response to the candidate. When the candidate says something not provided for in the framework, the examiner will allow the conversation to develop naturally. When this happens because the candidate has misunderstood, no indication will be given, but the examiner may try the question again at a later stage. If the candidate responds to the picture in Part 3 in such a way that the framework for Part 4 is irrelevant, the examiner will try to lead the conversation so that it fits the language tasks for that part even though it does not match the subject matter.

Timing is the responsibility of the examiner. Candidates need not worry about it.

Part 1

General conversation

This part of the test will be much the same for all candidates. It is designed to enable candidates to become used to the test situation and to help them overcome nervousness by dealing with very familiar areas of language. Although it is a 'warming-up' phase, it is fully assessed. The candidate must be able to give personal information, including spelling out one word. With paired candidates, they are asked to exchange information about themselves as if they did not already know each other. The examiner will ask each of them to spell out a word. For both paired and individual candidates, top marks go to those who show the ability to initiate parts of the conversation, rather than merely respond accurately to questions.

Preparing students

- This part of the test will be easy for students who have had plenty of practice in talking about themselves.

- Encourage students to learn to describe their homes, families, school, workplace, hobbies, etc. in English. Make sure they know any appropriate vocabulary.
- Use pair practice in the classroom so that students are used to asking and giving such information.

Part 2

Simulated situation

Candidates are asked to perform a simple role simulation with the examiner or fellow student. The examiner describes the situation and, usually, gives the candidate(s) a visual prompt, which may be a picture or a short piece of written material, for example a timetable or menu. The candidate(s) have a few moments' preparation time before they have to speak. It is quite in order for candidates to check that they have correctly understood the instructions before they begin, by, for example, repeating what they have been asked to do.

Preparing students

- Materials for simple role simulations are to found in many textbooks and full use should be made of these.
- The language needed for making plans and suggestions, for agreeing and disagreeing politely should be taught.
- Ways of asking for clarification and/or repetition should also be taught (e.g. 'I'm sorry, I didn't quite catch that. Could you repeat it please?'). Candidates are not penalised for occasionally making such a request, whether to the examiner or their partner in a pair test.

Part 3

Responding to a visual stimulus

The candidate is asked to describe and respond to a picture, normally a colour photograph. Lack of specialised vocabulary is not penalised, but good candidates will be expected to use paraphrasing where appropriate. There is no penalty for idiosyncratic interpretations of pictures, but candidates must be prepared to justify them. For example 'I think this is London because the traffic is busy', is fine, even if the picture shows New York! In pair tests, each candidate is given a different but related photograph. The photographs are returned to the examiner at the end of Part 3.

Preparing students

- Students should be equipped with the basic vocabulary for describing pictures of people and places. Preposition work is especially useful here, for locating and relating elements of the picture (behind, beside, on top of).
- Appropriate structures such as the use of the present continuous (e.g. 'The boy is serving a customer') and identifying phrases (e.g. 'the girl standing at the counter') should also be taught.
- Paraphrasing forms (e.g. 'the thing you use to change the programme on the television') should be well-practised, so that students are not unsettled by encountering objects they cannot name.

Part 4

General conversation following on from the photographs

Here the candidates are led to give information and opinions in a general conversation related to the photograph(s) in Part 3, without time being allowed for preparation. The examiner will normally offer personal information or opinions for the candidate to respond to.

Preparing students

- Students should practise giving personal opinions on a range of topics and narrating simple personal anecdotes.
- Classroom practice in groups or pairs can be developed as a game, where students are given subjects at random to comment on or relate a story about, incorporating a particular word or structure.
- Students should also be encouraged to listen to each other and learn how to offer appropriate comments on what they hear (e.g. 'Well, I don't really agree with you because ...').

Frameworks for the Speaking test

There are five Individual and five Pair frameworks. All the pictures etc. referred to are in the Colour Section in the Student's Book (see pages I–VIII).

Test 1

TEST 1   INDIVIDUAL (see pages 10–13 for more information)

Part 1

Tasks: Identifying oneself, giving information about people/things
Sub tasks: Spelling, numbers, responding to questions/information
Framework   (Where a pause is indicated, allow a few seconds, then prompt if no response is forthcoming.)

Teacher:

Please sit down. What's your name?

....

Can you tell me how old you are?

....

Where do you come from?

....

(if local)   (if another place)
So you know this area well. What part   *So you're a long way / not far*
of … do you live in exactly?   *from home. (Pause … prompt)*

....

Can you spell that, please?   *What is your street called?*

....

(Write down and repeat)
                                                    Can you spell that, please?
I don't know   *I think I know*
where that is.   *where that is.*   ....

....   (Write down and repeat)

And when did you begin studying English?

....

Are you learning English for a special purpose or for fun or … ?

....

14

(React – continue conversation if time allows)

Thank you.

Time: About two minutes.

TEST 1   INDIVIDUAL

Part 2

Tasks: Giving information about events, making plans

Framework Teacher (slowly):

I'm going to describe a situation to you.

We are visiting an adventure park.

(Indicate leaflet 1B to the student)

Here are some of the things you can do there. Please tell me what you'd like to do and at what time we can do each thing.

Just think for a few seconds.

Is that all right? Shall I repeat it?

(Pause)

So, what shall we do first?

....

How long does it last?

....

And then what?

....

What time will that start?

....

Do you think we'll have time for everything?

....

Well, it sounds like we're going to have a great day!

NB The task is achieved provided the student and teacher have an appropriate conversation consisting of about four exchanges based on the information given, even if the student omits one of the activities or adds extra ideas so that the conversation does not follow the pattern above.

Time: About two minutes.

TEST 1   INDIVIDUAL

Part 3

Tasks: Describing people and places, saying where people and things
                  are and what people are doing

Framework   Teacher (Indicate photo 1C to the student)

                  *Here is a photograph of someone working in a shop. Now, I'd
                  like you to look at it and tell me about it.*

                  If it seems necessary to intervene, use prompts rather than direct
                  questions if possible, e.g. *The clothes look rather expensive, I
                  think.*

                  The student should talk about the photograph for about one
                  minute or so, with little or no help from the teacher. It is not
                  expected that students should know the name of everything in
                  the photograph, but for a good mark they should be able to
                  paraphrase, e.g. they may not know the word 'tape measure'
                  but they should be able to say 'something to check the
                  customer's size' instead.

                  (Put the photograph aside before moving on to Part 4.)

TEST 1   INDIVIDUAL

Part 4

Tasks: Expressing opinions, stating preferences

Framework   Teacher:

                  Do you ever buy clothes in that sort of shop? Why / Why not?

                  Say something about your own shopping experiences, e.g. *I
                  once bought a very expensive coat. Then, when I looked at
                  myself in the mirror at home, I didn't like it at all! Have you
                  ever made a mistake when you were buying clothes?*

                  The student should give reasons for his/her opinion and talk
                  about a shopping experience, with little or no help from the
                  teacher.

Time: About four minutes for Part 3 and 4 together.

TEST 1   PAIR (see pages 10–13 for more information)

Part 1

Tasks: Identifying oneself, giving information about people/things, asking direct questions

Sub tasks: Spelling, numbers, responding to questions/information

Framework   Teacher:

Please sit down.

What are your names?

....

Do you know each other?

....

(if yes)   (if no)

Imagine/pretend you don't know each other and find out some information about each other.   *Find out some information about each other.*

The students' exchange should consist of about four or five turns each. If necessary, prompt to elicit information on home town, schools, jobs, family, etc. Select a suitable word for spelling from each student and ask for it at the end of the exchange, e.g. *Marie, you said you come from Toulouse. How do you spell that?*

(Thank the students and move on to Part 2.)

Time: About two or three minutes.

TEST 1   PAIR

Part 2

Tasks: Giving information about events, making plans

Framework   Teacher (slowly):

I'm going to describe a situation to you.

You are visiting an adventure park.

(Indicate leaflet 1A to Student A and leaflet 1B to Student B)

Here are some of the things you can do there, with their times. Decide together which things you'd like to do and when.

Just think for a few seconds.

Is that all right? Shall I repeat it?

(Pause)

Ready? Student A, would you like to start?

Allow students to complete the task without interrupting them unless absolutely necessary. After about two minutes, bring the discussion to a close with an appropriate remark, such as: *Well, it sounds like you're going to have a great day!*

NB The task is achieved if the students agree any reasonable plan without prompting.

Time: About two or three minutes (including time to assimilate the information).

TEST 1 PAIR

Part 3

Tasks: Describing people and places, saying where people and things are and what people are doing

Framework Teacher (to both students):

Now, I'm going to give each of you a photograph of someone working in a shop.

(Indicate photo 1C to Student A)

Student A, here is yours. Would you show it to Student B and tell him/her about it, please? Student B, I'll give you your photograph in a moment. Student A, would you start now? .... Thank you.

If it seems necessary to intervene, use prompts rather than direct questions if possible, e.g. *The clothes look rather expensive, I think.*

(Indicate photo 1D to Student B)

Student B, here is your photograph. Would you show it to Student A and tell him/her about it, please?

Pause for a moment.

Are you ready? .... Thank you.

Each student should talk about the photograph for about one minute or so, with little or no help from the teacher. It is not expected that students should know the name of everything in the photograph, but for a good mark they should be able to paraphrase, e.g. they may not know the word 'tape measure' but they should be able to say 'something to check the customer's size' instead.

(Put the photographs aside before moving to Part 4.)

TEST 1 PAIR

Part 4

Tasks: Expressing opinions, stating preferences

Framework   Teacher (to both students):

Talk to each other about the sort of shops you like to buy clothes in and the sort of clothes you like. Find out whether your partner spends a lot of time choosing clothes.

The students should give reasons for their opinions and talk about choosing clothes, with little or no help from the teacher.

Time: About five minutes for Parts 3 and 4 together.

Test 2

TEST 2   INDIVIDUAL (see pages 10–13 for more information)

Part 1

Tasks: Identifying oneself, giving information about things

Sub tasks: Spelling, numbers, responding to questions/information

Framework (Where a pause is indicated, allow a few seconds, then prompt if no response is forthcoming.)

Teacher:

Please sit down. What's your name?

....

Where do you come from?

....

Can you spell that for me, please?

I've never been to … (Pause … prompt)	*I was there ten years ago. (Pause … prompt)*
....	....
What is it like?	*Has it changed much?*
....	....

Have you lived there for a long time?

....

Why are you learning English? For your job, or for fun or … ?

....

(React – continue conversation if time allows)

Thank you.

Time: About two minutes.

TEST 2   INDIVIDUAL

Part 2

Tasks: Making suggestions, giving reasons for choices

Framework Teacher (slowly):

I'm going to describe a situation to you.

A friend of yours is going abroad for a year. You want to give him/her a present.

(Indicate picture 2A to the student)

Here are some suggestions for presents. Please tell me which ones would be suitable and which would not be.

Just think for a few seconds.

Is that all right? Shall I repeat it?

(Pause)

So, what do you suggest?

....

Why do you think that would be best?

....

Is there anything else you think would be all right?

....

What about (item not mentioned)?

....

Why / Why not?

....

Anyway, I'm sure your friend will be very pleased!

NB The task is achieved provided the student and teacher have an appropriate conversation consisting of about four exchanges based on the information given, even if the student omits some items or adds extra ideas so that the conversation does not follow the pattern above.

Time: About two minutes.

TEST 2   INDIVIDUAL

Part 3

Tasks: Describing people and places, saying where people and things are and what people are doing

Framework Teacher (Indicate photo 2B to the student)

Here is a photograph of some people on a canal boat. Now, I'd like you to look at it and tell me about it.

If it seems necessary to intervene, use prompts rather than direct questions if possible, e.g. *It looks <u>very relaxing to me</u>.*

The student should talk about the photograph for about one minute or so, with little or no help from the teacher. It is not expected that students should know the name of everything in the photograph, but for a good mark they should be able to paraphrase, e.g. they may not know the word 'steer' but they should be able to say 'control the direction of the boat' instead.

(Put the photograph aside before moving on to Part 4.)

TEST 2   INDIVIDUAL

Part 4

Tasks:	Expressing opinions, stating preferences
Framework	Teacher:

Do you think you would like a holiday on a canal boat? Why/Why not?

Say something about a holiday experience of your own, e.g. *I had a wonderful holiday cycling round France last year. What's the best holiday you've ever had?*

The student should give reasons for his/her opinion and talk about a holiday, with little or no help from the teacher.

Time:	About four minutes for Parts 3 and 4 together.

TEST 2   PAIR (see pages 10–13 for more information)

Part 1

Tasks: Identifying oneself, giving information about people/things, asking direct questions

Sub tasks: Spelling, numbers, responding to questions/information

Framework   Teacher:

Please sit down.

What are your names?

....

Do you know each other?

....

(if yes)   (if no)

Imagine/pretend you   *Find out some information*
don't know each other   *about each other.*
and find out some
information about each
other.

The students' exchange should consist of about four or five turns each. If necessary, prompt to elicit information on home town, schools, jobs, family, etc. Select a suitable word for spelling from each student and ask for it at the end of the exchange, e.g. *Andreas, you said your family is from Zurich. How do you spell that?*

(Thank the students and move on to Part 2.)

Time: About two or three minutes.

TEST 2   PAIR

Part 2

Tasks: Making suggestions, giving reasons for choices

Framework   Teacher (slowly):

I'm going to describe a situation to you.

A friend of yours is going abroad for a year. You want to give him/her a present.

(Indicate picture 2A to both students)

Here are some suggestions for presents. Decide together which would be most suitable for your friend and which would not be. Tell each other your reasons.

Just think for a few seconds.

Is that all right? Shall I repeat it?

(Pause)

Ready? Student A, would you like to start?

Allow students to complete the task without interrupting them unless absolutely necessary. After about two minutes, bring the discussion to a close with an appropriate remark, such as: *Well, I'm sure your friend will be very pleased with the present.*

NB The task is achieved if the students exchange opinions on both suitable and unsuitable presents and give their reasons.

Time: About two or three minutes (including time to assimilate the information).

TEST 2 PAIR

Part 3

Tasks: Describing people and places, saying where people and things are and what people are doing

Framework Teacher (to both students):

Now, I'm going to give each of you a photograph of some people on boats.

(Indicate photo 2B to Student A)

Student A, here is yours. They're on a canal boat. Would you show it to Student B and tell him/her about it, please? Student B, I'll give you your photograph in a moment. Student A, would you start now? .... Thank you.

If it seems necessary to intervene, use prompts rather than direct questions if possible, e.g. *It looks very relaxing to me.*

(Indicate photo 2C to Student B)

Student B, here is your photograph. They're on a sailing boat. Would you show it to Student A and tell him/her about it, please?

Pause for a moment.

Are you ready? .... Thank you.

Each student should talk about the photograph for about one minute or so, with little or no help from the teacher. It is not expected that students should know the name of everything in the photograph, but for a good mark they should be able to paraphrase, e.g. they may not know the word 'steer' but they should be able to say 'control the direction of the boat' instead.

(Put the photographs aside before moving on to Part 4.)

TEST 2   PAIR

Part 4

Tasks: Expressing opinions, stating preferences

Framework   Teacher (to both students):

Talk to each other about the sort of things you like to do on holiday and the places you like to go to. Find out whether your partner likes to try new activities on holiday.

The students should give reasons for their opinions and talk about holiday activities, with little or no help from the teacher.

Time: About five minutes for Parts 3 and 4 together.

Test 3

TEST 3   INDIVIDUAL (see pages 10–13 for more information)

Part 1

Tasks:	Identifying oneself, giving information about things
Sub tasks:	Spelling, numbers, responding to questions/information
Framework	(Where a pause is indicated, allow a few seconds, then prompt if no response is forthcoming.)

Teacher:

Please sit down. What's your name?

....

Are you a full-time student or do you have a job?

....

(if still at school)   (if working)

What is your favourite subject? ?   *I don't know much about … (Pause …
                                                        prompt)* ....

*What do you particularly like
about … ?*   *What sort of things do you have to
                                                        do?*

....

You mentioned … Can you spell that, please ?

....

(Write down and repeat)
And what are your plans for the future?

....

So how useful/important will English be for you?

....

(React – continue conversation if time allows)
Thank you.

Time:	About two minutes.

TEST 3   INDIVIDUAL

Part 2

Tasks:	Inviting, making plans
Framework	Teacher (slowly):

I'm going to describe a situation to you.
You want to invite me to come swimming with you.
(Indicate leaflet 3A to the student)

Here are the opening times of the swimming pool. Please phone me and ask me to come swimming one day next week.

Just think for a few seconds.

Is that all right? Shall I repeat it?

(Pause)

(answering phone) *Hello?*

....

Well, I'd love to come with you, but I'm quite busy next week. Which day do you want to go?

....

And what time?

....

That's difficult for me. Is there any other time we could go?

....

That's better. So where do you want to meet?

....

Fine. I'll see you there at … o'clock.

NB The task is achieved provided the student and teacher have an appropriate conversation consisting of about four exchanges based on the information given, even if the student omits some information or adds extra ideas so that the conversation does not follow the pattern above.

Time: About two minutes.

TEST 3   INDIVIDUAL

Part 3

Tasks: Describing objects and places, saying where objects and things are

Framework   Teacher (Indicate photo 3C to the student)

Here is a photograph of a room. Now, I'd like you to look at it and tell me about it.

If it seems necessary to intervene, use prompts rather than direct questions if possible, e.g. *The person who lives there must be very tidy.*

The student should talk about the photograph for about one minute or so, with little or no help from the teacher. It is not expected that students should know the name of everything in the photograph, but for a good mark they should be able to paraphrase, e.g. they may not know the word 'patio' but they should be able to say 'a place where you can sit outside' instead.

(Put the photograph aside before moving on to Part 4.)

TEST 3   INDIVIDUAL

Part 4

Tasks:	Expressing opinions, describing experiences
Framework	Teacher:

Would you like your living room furnished like this? Why / Why not?

Say something about your own experiences, e.g. *I was visiting some friends once and I spilt some coffee on their new white carpet. Have you ever done anything like that? How did you feel?*

The student should talk about his/her tastes and describe an experience, with little or no help from the teacher.

Time:	About four minutes for Parts 3 and 4 together.

Part 1

Tasks:	Identifying oneself, giving information about people/things, asking direct questions
Sub tasks:	Spelling, numbers, responding to questions/information
Framework	Teacher:

Please sit down.

What are your names?

....

Do you know each other?

....

(if yes)

Imagine/pretend you don't know each other and find out some information about each other.

(if no)

Find out some information about each other.

The students' exchange should consist of about four or five turns each. If necessary, prompt to elicit information on home town, schools, jobs, family, etc. Select a suitable word for spelling from each student and ask for it at the end of the exchange, e.g. *Anna, you said your family name was Weiss. How do you spell that?*

(Thank the students and move on to Part 2.)

Time:	About two or three minutes.

Part 2

Tasks:	Inviting, making plans
Framework	Teacher (slowly):

I'm going to describe a situation to you.

Student A, you want to go swimming next week and you are telephoning Student B to invite him/her to come with you. Here is some information about the swimming pool.

(Indicate leaflet 3A to Student A)

Student B, here is your diary for next week.

(Indicate diary 3B to Student B)

Discuss which day you'll go and what time.

Just think for a few seconds.

Is that all right? Shall I repeat it?

(Pause)

Ready? Student A, would you like to start by inviting Student B?

Allow students to complete the task without interrupting them unless absolutely necessary. After about two minutes, bring the discussion to a close with an appropriate remark, such as: *Well, I hope you enjoy your swim.*

NB The task is achieved if the students agree any reasonable arrangement.

Time: About two or three minutes (including time to assimilate the information).

TEST 3 PAIR

Part 3

Tasks: Describing objects and places, saying where objects and things are

Framework Teacher (to both students):

Now, I'm going to give each of you a photograph of a room.

(Indicate photo 3C to Student A)

Student A, here is yours. Would you show it to Student B and tell him/her about it, please? Student B, I'll give you your photograph in a moment. Student A, would you start now? .... Thank you.

If it seems necessary to intervene, use prompts rather than direct questions if possible, e.g. *The person who lives there must be very tidy.*

(Indicate photo 3D to Student B)

Student B, here is your photograph. Would you show it to Student A and tell him/her about it, please?

Pause for a moment.

Are you ready? .... Thank you.

Each student should talk about the photograph for about one minute or so, with little or no help from the teacher. It is not expected that students should know the name of everything in the photograph, but for a good mark they should be able to paraphrase, e.g. they may not know the word 'patio' but they should be able to say 'a place where you can sit outside' instead.

(Put the photographs aside before moving on to Part 4.)

Part 4

Tasks:	Expressing opinions, describing preferences
Framework	Teacher (to both students):

Talk to each other about the sort of houses and furniture you like. Find out whether your partner prefers any particular style.

The students should give reasons for their opinions and talk about houses and furniture, with little or no help from the teacher.

Time:	About five minutes for Parts 3 and 4 together.

Test 4

TEST 4   INDIVIDUAL (see pages 10–13 for more information)

Part 1

Tasks:	Identifying oneself, giving information about things
Sub tasks:	Spelling, numbers, responding to questions/information
Framework	(Where a pause is indicated, allow a few seconds, then prompt if no response is forthcoming.)

Teacher:

Please sit down. What's your name?

....

Where are you studying? / Which school do you go to?

....

I haven't heard of that. / I'm not sure if I know that one. Can you spell the name for me, please?

....

(Write down and repeat)
Have you studied English anywhere else?

....

(React – continue conversation if time allows)
Thank you.

Time:	About two minutes.

TEST 4   INDIVIDUAL

Part 2

Tasks:	Giving opinions, making plans
Framework	Teacher (slowly):

I'm going to describe a situation to you.
We are going out for dinner this evening with some friends.
(Indicate advertisements 4A and 4B to the student)
Here are advertisements for two restaurants. Please tell me which one you think we should go to.
Just think for a few seconds.
Is that all right? Shall I repeat it?
(Pause)
So, where shall we go?

....

Why did you choose that one?

....

You don't think it might be too noisy/expensive (as appropriate)?

....

OK. So, do you think we should book a table?

....

What time do you think we should go?

....

All right. That's fine for me.

NB The task is achieved provided the student and teacher have an appropriate conversation consisting of about four exchanges based on the information given, even if the student omits one of the activities or adds extra ideas so that the conversation does not follow the pattern above.

Time: About two minutes.

TEST 4   INDIVIDUAL

Part 3

Tasks: Describing people and places, saying where people and things are and what people are doing

Framework   Teacher (Indicate photo 4C to the student)

Here is a photograph of a hospital room. Now, I'd like you to look at it and tell me about it.

If it seems necessary to intervene, use prompts rather than direct questions if possible, e.g. *The <u>nurse looks friendly</u>.*

The student should talk about the photograph for about one minute or so, with little or no help from the teacher. It is not expected that students should know the name of everything in the photograph, but for a good mark they should be able to paraphrase, e.g. they may not know the word 'patient' but they should be able to say 'the person who is ill' instead.

(Put the photograph aside before moving on to Part 4.)

TEST 4   INDIVIDUAL

Part 4

Tasks: Expressing opinions, describing a general situation

Framework Teacher:

Would you like to do this sort of job? Why / Why not?

Say something about the experience of people working in medicine, e.g. *My brother is a doctor in England. He works terribly long hours and says he isn't paid enough. What can you tell me about doctors in your country?*

The student should give reasons for his/her opinion and say something about working in medicine, with little or no help from the teacher.

Time: About four minutes for Parts 3 and 4 together.

TEST 4   PAIR (see pages 10–13 for more information)

Part 1

Tasks: Identifying oneself, giving information about people/things, asking direct questions

Sub tasks: Spelling, numbers, responding to questions/information

Framework   Teacher:

Please sit down.

What are your names?

....

Do you know each other?

....

(if yes)   (if no)

Imagine/pretend you   *Find out some information*
don't know each other   *about each other.*
and find out some
information about each
other.

The students' exchange should consist of about four or five turns each. If necessary, prompt to elicit information on home town, schools, jobs, family etc. Select a suitable word for spelling from each student and ask for it at the end of the exchange, e.g. *Fernando, you said you were at the Newtown Academy. How do you spell Newtown?*

(Thank the students and move on to Part 2.)

Time: About two or three minutes.

TEST 4   PAIR

Part 2

Tasks: Giving information, making plans

Framework

Teacher (slowly):

I'm going to describe a situation to you.

You have decided to go out for a meal together and you are talking on the telephone about where you will go. Student A, you have seen this advertisement.

(Indicate advertisement 4A to Student A)

Student B, you have seen this advertisement.

(Indicate advertisement 4B to Student B)

Tell each other the good things about the restaurants and discuss which one to go to.

Just think for a few seconds.

Is that all right? Shall I repeat it?

(Pause)

Ready? Student A, would you like to start?

Allow students to complete the task without interrupting them unless absolutely necessary. After about two minutes, bring the discussion to a close with an appropriate remark, such as: *Well, I hope you enjoy your meal.*

NB The task is achieved if the students agree which restaurant to go to.

Time: About two or three minutes (including time to assimilate the information).

TEST 4   PAIR

Part 3

Tasks: Describing people and places, saying where people and things are and what people are doing

Framework   Teacher (to both students):

Now, I'm going to give each of you a photograph of a room in a hospital.

(Indicate photo 4C to Student A)

Student A, here is yours. Would you show it to Student B and tell him/her about it, please? Student B, I'll give you your photograph in a moment. Student A, would you start now? .... *Thank you.*

If it seems necessary to intervene, use prompts rather than direct questions if possible, e.g. *The nurse looks friendly.*

(Indicate photo 4D to Student B)

Student B, here is your photograph. Would you show it to Student A and tell him/her about it, please?

Pause for a moment.

Are you ready? .... *Thank you.*

Each student should talk about the photograph for about one minute or so, with little or no help from the teacher. It is not expected that students should know the name of everything in the photograph, but for a good mark they should be able to paraphrase, e.g. they may not know the word 'patient' but they should be able to say 'the person who is ill' instead.

(Put the photographs aside before moving on to Part 4.)

Part 4

Tasks: Expressing and explaining opinions

Framework   Teacher (to both students):

Find out from each other about whether your partner would like to work as a doctor or a nurse and ask them why, or why not. Is it a good job in your country(ies)?

The students should give reasons for their opinions and talk about working in medicine, with little or no help from the teacher.

Time: About five minutes for Parts 3 and 4 together.

Test 5

INDIVIDUAL (see pages 10–13 for more information)

Part 1

Tasks:	Identifying oneself, giving information about things
Sub tasks:	Spelling, numbers, responding to questions/information
Framework	(Where a pause is indicated, allow a few seconds, then prompt if no response is forthcoming.)

Teacher:

Please sit down. What's your name?

....

Do you come from this area? / Where do you come from?

....

So your first language is … (Pause … prompt)

....

Can you spell that for me, please?

....

Have you been learning English for a long time?

....

And do you have a particular reason for learning English?
(React – continue conversation if time allows)
Thank you.

Time:	About two minutes.

INDIVIDUAL

Part 2

Tasks:	Talking about places, making plans
Framework	Teacher (slowly):

I'm going to describe a situation to you.
We are spending a day in a town called Bellingham.
(Indicate map 5A to the student)
Here is a map of the town.
Please tell me which places you'd like to see.
Just think for a few seconds.
Is that all right? Shall I repeat it?
(Pause)
So, where shall we go first?

....

That's a good idea. How long do you think we'll spend there?

....

Yes, I agree. And then what shall we do?

....

Shall we walk or get a bus?

....

OK. And what shall we do for lunch? It looks like there are several possibilities …

....

Well, I think we're going to have a very good time!

NB The task is achieved provided the student and teacher have an appropriate conversation consisting of about four exchanges based on the information given, even if the student omits one of the activities or adds extra ideas so that the conversation does not follow the pattern above.

Time: About two minutes.

TEST 5   INDIVIDUAL

Part 3

Tasks: Describing people and places, saying where people and things are and what people are doing

Framework   Teacher (Indicate photo 5B to the student)

Here is a photograph of some language students in a laboratory. Now, I'd like you to look at it and tell me about it.

If it seems necessary to intervene, use prompts rather than direct questions if possible, e.g. *They all seem to be working very hard.*

The student should talk about the photograph for about one minute or so, with little or no help from the teacher. It is not expected that students should know the name of everything in the photograph, but for a good mark they should be able to paraphrase, e.g. they may not know the word 'headphones' but they should be able to say 'the thing on your head you hear through' instead.

(Put the photograph aside before moving on to Part 4.)

TEST 5   INDIVIDUAL

Part 4

Tasks:	Expressing opinions, stating preferences
Framework	Teacher:

Have you ever studied in a language laboratory? Do you like the idea? Why / Why not?

Say something about your own learning experiences, e.g. I studied French for seven years at school but I couldn't understand anything until I went to France. What do you think is the best way to study a language?

The student should give reasons for his/her opinion and talk about language learning, with little or no help from the teacher.

Time:	About four minutes for Parts 3 and 4 together.

(see pages 10–13 for more information)

Part 1

Tasks:	Identifying oneself, giving information about people/things, asking direct questions
Sub tasks:	Spelling, numbers, responding to questions/information
Framework	Teacher:

Please sit down.

What are your names?

....

Do you know each other?

....

(if yes)

Imagine/pretend you don't know each other and find out some information about each other.

(if no)

Find out some information about each other.

The students' exchange should consist of about four or five turns each. If necessary, prompt to elicit information on home town, schools, jobs, family, etc. Select a suitable word for spelling from each student and ask for it at the end of the exchange, e.g. *Mariam, you said you live in Alveston Road. How do you spell that?*

(Thank the students and move on to Part 2.)

Time:	About two or three minutes.

Part 2

Tasks:	Talking about places, making plans
Framework	Teacher (slowly):

I'm going to describe a situation to you.

You have decided to spend a day out in a town called Bellingham.

(Indicate map 5A to both students)

Here is a map of the town. Talk about the places you'd like to go to; which one you'll go to first, which one next, and so on; where you'll go for lunch; how you will get around.

Just think for a few seconds.

Is that all right? Shall I repeat it?

(Pause)

Ready? Student A, would you like to start?

Allow students to complete the task without interrupting them unless absolutely necessary. After about two minutes, bring the discussion to a close with an appropriate remark, such as: *Well, I hope you enjoy your day out.*

NB The task is achieved if the students agree on where to go.

Time: About two or three minutes (including time to assimilate the information).

TEST 5 PAIR

Part 3

Tasks: Describing people and places, saying where people and things are and what people are doing

Framework   Teacher (to both students):

Now, I'm going to give each of you a photograph of some language students.

(Indicate photo 5B to Student A)

Student A, here is yours. Would you show it to Student B and tell him/her about it, please? Student B, I'll give you your photograph in a moment. Student A, would you start now? .... Thank you.

If it seems necessary to intervene, use prompts rather than direct questions if possible, e.g. *They all seem to be working very hard.*

(Indicate photo 5C to Student B)

Student B, here is your photograph. Would you show it to Student A and tell him/her about it, please?

Pause for a moment.

Are you ready? .... Thank you.

Each student should talk about the photograph for about one minute or so, with little or no help from the teacher. It is not expected that students should know the name of everything in the photograph, but for a good mark they should be able to paraphrase, e.g. they may not know the word 'headphones' but they should be able to say 'the thing on your head you hear through' instead.

(Put the photographs aside before moving on to Part 4.)

Part 4

Tasks: Expressing opinions, stating preferences

Framework Teacher (to both students):

Talk to each other about different ways of studying foreign languages. Find out what your partner thinks is the best way to study.

The students should give reasons for their opinions and talk about studying languages, with little or no help from the teacher.

Time: About five minutes for Parts 3 and 4 together.

Recording answers

Answers for the Reading, Writing and Listening Papers are recorded on computerised answer sheets which are marked by OMR (Optical Mark Reader). There are samples for each part in the Student's Book which may be photocopied without further permission. Teachers should encourage students to use these whenever they use the Practice Tests, so that students are perfectly familiar with them and are not distracted by worrying about them during the real test. All answers should be written *in pencil*. This is especially important as the OMR is not sensitive to ink. Students should be used to rubbing out cleanly with an eraser, if they wish to change an answer and should be reminded to take one into the examination room with their pencils. Correcting fluid should not be used.

Reading

For this paper, students fill in the lozenges on the OMR sheet to show which answer they have chosen. These pencil marks will be read by the OMR. It is best for students to become used to marking their answers directly onto the OMR sheets as they work through the test. This saves time and avoids the possibility of making copying errors under pressure. Students should be careful not to record answers against the wrong question number, especially if they leave a question unanswered. They should be reminded that no blanks should be left, as guesses may be correct, whereas blanks cannot be.

Writing

This paper is examiner marked, but OMR sheets are used to ensure fast and accurate recording of marks. Students should practise writing their answers clearly in the spaces provided. Some students with large handwriting may need to modify it to ensure that they can fit their answers comfortably in the space available. Most students will probably want to try out answers to Parts 1 and 2 on the question paper before writing on the OMR sheet, but they should be trained to check very carefully to avoid copying errors. For Part 1, students should be reassured that it is *not* necessary to copy the beginning of each sentence onto the answer sheet. For Part 2, only the answer need be transferred. For Part 3, students should be encouraged to use the space on the question paper for *planning*, but to write their final letter straight onto the OMR sheet.

Listening

While listening, candidates can mark their answers onto the question paper. At the end of the test, twelve minutes is allowed for the transfer of answers to the OMR sheet. This is very generous and allows for very careful checking that all answers have been transferred correctly. Parts 1, 2 and 4 are answered by filling in lozenges, as with the Reading paper. For Part 3, only the words of the answers should be transferred, not the phrases given on the question paper.

Marking and grading

Marking

Each of the four components (Reading, Writing, Listening and Speaking) of the PET carries 25 per cent of the marks. The final mark is an aggregate of the marks obtained in each of the four components. There is no minimum pass mark for individual components. Candidates need to score approximately 70 per cent overall in order to pass.

Reading

There are 35 raw marks which are then weighted to 25.

Writing

This part of the exam is marked by EFL examiners who are trained and monitored. The mark scheme for each question details possible alternative answers. Parts 1 and 2 allow one mark per question. For Part 3, examiners use the assessment criteria shown on page 46.

Listening

Each question carries one mark.

Speaking

Candidates are assessed by two examiners who award a mark out of 25 according to the requirements shown on page 53.

The results slip

PET has two passing and two failing grades: pass with merit, pass, narrow fail, fail. The grade is shown on the results slip.

Mark scheme for Writing Part 3

There are ten marks for this part. The five marks for task always include one mark for length, one mark for signing off appropriately and three marks for covering points outlined in the rubric. The five marks for language are awarded for accurate use of a range of vocabulary and structures appropriate to the task. NB All of these comments should be interpreted *at PET level.*

Mark	Task	Language
5	Very good attempt at task, including all required content in full with little no digression. Generally coherent, or requiring no effort by the reader.	Generally good control, and confident use of PET language. Coherent linking of sentences using simple cohesive devices. Language includes complex sentences and a range of structures and vocabulary. Language errors may still be present, but they are minor, due to ambition, and do not impede communication.
4	Good attempt at task, covering all the content elements, with some elaboration. There may be some minor repetition or digression, though overall reasonably coherent and requiring minimal effort on the part of the reader.	Reasonable control of language and linking of sentences. Language is either unambitious (i.e. avoiding complex structures and using a narrow range of vocabulary) but accurate, or ambitious (i.e. attempting a range of structures and vocabulary) but with some errors, although the errors do not generally impede communication.
3	Reasonable attempt at task. May be a rather simple account with little elaboration, or a fuller attempt combining some repetition or digression. One significant element of required content may have been omitted. Coherent enough to make meaning clear, although a little effort may be required by the reader.	Evidence of some control of language, and simple sentence structure generally sound. Language likely to be unambitious, or if ambitious probably flawed. A number of errors may be present, e.g. in structures, tenses, spelling, articles, prepositions, but they do not generally impede communication. Linking of sentences not always maintained.
2	Some attempt at task, possibly indicating limited understanding of what is required. Two elements of required content may have been omitted, or there will be noticeable irrelevance or incoherence, which will require considerable effort by the reader. The task may be unfinished.	Erratic control of sentence structure and use of tenses, e.g. past simple not used appropriately in many cases. Language may be very simplistic / limited / repetitive. Errors in the spelling of PET vocabulary often occur. Language errors will impede communication at times. Punctuation may be noticeably absent, leading to incoherence of sentences.
1	Poor attempt at task, including little of relevance, and/or it is far too short or very incoherent.	Very poor control of language. Difficult to understand due to frequent errors in areas such as grammar, spelling or sentence construction. There may be a general absence of punctuation, leading to serious incoherence.
0	Candidate has misunderstood or misinterpreted task. Content bears no relation to task.	Achieves nothing. Language impossible to understand.

Note: The wording of this UCLES mark scheme has been amended slightly to avoid specialist terminology.

PET Writing Part 3 – marked sample answers

The following samples have been selected from students' answers produced during trialling and have been marked in accordance with the Mark Scheme on page 46 in order to help teachers in assessing the work of their own students. Brief explanatory notes have been added to show how the marks were arrived at.

NB These are not model answers and should not be used as such in the classroom.

SAMPLE A

Test 5

> Dear Cecy,
>   I am writing to tell you about my trip abroad last month.
>   First of all I would like to tell you that it was an incredable experience because I had the chance to visit many places and meet a lot of people.
>   I went to Madrid, and as I have some family there, Christmas Eve was very nice. I visited El Prado museum and walked around the city, I also had the chance to visit Toledo which is a beautiful town. We had sunshine everyday, even when the temperature was minus 0 C.
>   Well, what about going to Venezuela next summer together? Think about it and write me back.
>   Best wishes,
>   XXXX

Task: 5 marks
This student has written a confident, well-organised letter, describing what she did and her reactions. Although she has not made direct use of the visual stimuli, she has mentioned a variety of details about her trip to give an all-round picture within the required word length and has ended her letter appropriately.

Language: 5 marks
Well-controlled and appropriate structures and vocabulary are used accurately with good linking. Language is ambitious and varied for PET level. Very minor errors.

Total: 10 marks out of a possible 10

SAMPLE B

Test 1

> Dear Alex .
>
> You'll be pleased you decided not to come on holiday with us when you hear what happened!
>
> We were in France going to Paris but Ernest forgot the Motorway's map, and we were lost, After 2 hours driving we found a small Town; where we asked a policeman: Where we are? But the policeman couldn't understand us. He couldn't speak English. We were hungry and started to look for a Restarrant, when the car broke down. But it isn't a big problem because we found a Mechanic in the Cafe, in Front of where we were. the Mechanic told us, He needs two days to repair it. We decided stay in a Hotel near there, the hotel wasn't very good, It was dirty and Expensive, but It was the Only hotel in the Town. When the car was ready, we went to Paris to have a beatifull holiday without money because the mechanic's bill was very Expensive and we decided came back home.
>
> I would like know about your holidays.
>
> Write to me soon.
>
> XXXX

Task: 4 marks
This student makes a good attempt at covering all the points and elaborating some of them. The narrative is coherent but too long with unnecessary details. It closes appropriately.

Language: 4 marks
The language is reasonably well-controlled with some attempt at linking and generally accurate and appropriate structures. Some minor errors, notably spelling and punctuation, which do not impede communication.

Total: 8 marks out of a possible 10

SAMPLE C

Test 1

> *Dear Cen,*
>
> *You'll be pleased you decided not to come on holiday with us when you hear what happened!*
>
> *When I were driving a car in the night sudenly my car has broke down. Our friends were very afraid because we have never been this town before. First time we thought we were lucky because we saw hotel and we could stay and after in the morning we could find some one for car. then – we went to the Hotel. There was a women in the reception She told she hadn't got any room so unfortunatly we slept in the car because there wasn't any hotel in the town.*
>
> *3 hours later when we were resting we saw cafe and we went there. but unfortunatly there wasn't any food in the cafe but shopkeeper was very friendly. He was understanding car so He repaired the car and after he gave us a cup of coffee. We told thanks after we got on our car and left there.*
>
> *I can tell you the other things about holiday when I come back.*
>
> *Yours sincerely*
>
> *XXXX*

Task: 4 marks
This student makes a good attempt at the task, producing a coherent narrative. The account is too long because too many minor, distracting details are introduced.

Language: 3 marks
Simple sentence structure is sound but errors occur when more ambitious language is attempted. Some good linking in places but elsewhere it is not even attempted.

Total: 7 marks out of a possible 10

SAMPLE D

Test 2

Dear **Matthias**,

I've just finished a short language course in Scotland and I want to tell you all about it.

I had lessons from Monday to Friday. One day was in the morning, another day was in the afternoon. When I didn't have a lesson, Language School gave me a lot of events. I played badminton on Monday afternoon. It has a small Sports Centre near it, so I did easily. On Tuesday I draw picture. Art teacher come to there once a week.

I went to Edinburgh Castle with my friends on Wednesday afternoon. They were very funny. We always laughed until the end of course. They already had gone to each mother countries. I spent in host family on Thursday morning. I wash dishes and my clothes. On Friday I went to museum. It was called "Scottish Royal MUSEUM". There were many historical things. I was interested in looking at them. I had excellent days in Scotand.

Thank you

Love from

XXXX

Task: 3 marks

This student makes a good attempt at the task. The reader's impression of her experiences is clear. She has used all the information given but in a very literal way. She gives each piece of information the same importance instead of organising it to give a more general picture and therefore writes too much.

Language: 3 marks

There is reasonable control of tenses with a few slips. There are few successful attempts at more ambitious structures. Control of articles and the use of transitive/intransitive verbs is poor but this does not generally impede communication.

Total: 6 marks out of a possible 10

SAMPLE E

Test 2

> Dear Tomohiro,
>
> I've just finished a short language course in Scotland and I want to tell you all about it.
>
> I stayed here for one week with English family. They were very friendly. There were three in this family. Their daughter was high school students. She often took me to interesting place in a holiday. In school, I could make a many friend in this school. My best friend is Paul comes from France. He has been studying English for three years. I've been learning English for six years. But he speaks English better than me. He is a same class as me. We often had a discussion in this class I realy enjoyed it and it was useful to learn English. I am looking forward to seeing you again
>
> love   XXXX

Task: 2 marks
This student's treatment of the task is uneven. Some aspects are treated in too much detail and others are barely touched on.

Language: 3 marks
Shows evidence of good control of basic structures although there is little attempt at linking. Language is unambitious and the errors, although fairly widespread, do not generally impede communication.

Total: 5 marks out of a possible 10

SAMPLE F

Test 4

Dear **Mr Stevens,**

I have seen your advertisement in the newspaper and I would very much like to work with you. **I am eighteen years old, and I am dynamic person. I like the contact with an other people. I talk three language: the English, the French, and the Spanish. I do a lot of Sports, exemple: the Basketball, Tennis ect ... In 1990, I aid for organiser an international conference in London, with many peoples, with the famaus Doctor X.**

My adress:
        45 ......
          ......
          ......
Goodbye
                XXXX

Task: 2 marks
This student has made some attempt at the task, giving some but not enough relevant information. There is some incoherence (e.g. 18 years old but organised conference several years ago). Too short.

Language: 2 marks
Poor control of sentence structure. No evidence of tense control. Incorrect spelling of PET level vocabulary. Some errors impede communication.

Total: 4 marks out of a possible 10

Assessing the Speaking test

Students' performance is assessed for both language skills (fluency, accuracy and appropriacy of language, and pronunciation) and task achievement (the ability to work towards a conclusion with as little intervention from the examiner as is reasonable). The total mark for the Speaking test is twenty (that is, five marks for each of the language skills and five for task achievement. This is scaled to represent 25 per cent of the marks for the PET as a whole.

UCLES offers the following explanation of what is required of PET candidates in each of these areas:

Fluency refers to the naturalness of the speed and rhythm of the utterances. At PET level, candidates are unlikely to produce language which is very fluent. However, it may be that some candidates will be fluent but grammatically inaccurate, or fluent but with poor pronunciation.

Accuracy and Appropriacy of Language refers to the range and accuracy of both the grammatical structures and vocabulary used.

Candidates are not expected to produce utterances without inaccuracies at PET level. Therefore, an assessment of a candidate's performance should be based on the way in which messages are conveyed in both grammatical and lexical terms: for example, a missing third person singular 's' is a minor error (e.g. 'He come to school every day'), but an utterance such as 'I stay here three months' may obscure meaning and therefore is assessed as a more serious inaccuracy. Similarly, candidates are not expected to know words such as 'easel' or 'filing tray' but reference to 'a sort of desk for painting on' or 'a tray for papers' would indicate top-level performance. The ability to paraphrase shows a flexibility of language and should be rewarded.

Pronunciation includes individual sounds, linking, prosodic features, rhythm and intonation.

The influence of first language pronunciation is quite normal. In awarding marks, examiners must assess whether a non-teaching native speaker with an average degree of patience could understand the candidate.

Task Achievement The mark for task achievement is a global one covering performance in each of the four sections. (In Part 1, for example, the task for candidates is to give and exchange information about themselves.) Even though the candidate's language performance may be at a low level according to the criteria, marks for task achievement should be awarded for the willingness to give information, take part in a stimulated situation, describe people and places and express a personal reaction.

Key

Test 1

Reading

Part 1 Questions 1–5

1 B   2 C   3 B   4 A   5 D

Part 2 Questions 6–10

6 E   7 A   8 C   9 H   10 F

Part 3 Questions 11–20

11 A   12 B   13 B   14 B   15 A   16 B   17 A   18 B
19 A   20 B

Part 4 Questions 21–25

21 C   22 A   23 A   24 C   25 B

Part 5 Questions 26–35

26 C   27 A   28 C   29 A   30 B   31 B   32 B
33 A   34 C   35 D

Writing

Part 1 Questions 1–5

1 was won by her team.
2 had done very well.
3 has (got) / 's got three teams.
4 for two years. / since two years ago.
5 has won fewer matches than the girls' (team). / hasn't won so/as many
   matches as the girls' (team). / has lost more matches than the girls' (team).

Part 2 Questions 6–15

Appropriate answers acceptable. For **14** any accurately expressed, appropriate
answer acceptable.

Part 3 Question 16

Task
Using a scale from 0–5, reward answers which include the following:
a) Description of what happened
b) Information about small town
c) Coherent narrative
d) Appropriate ending
e) Appropriate length

Language
Using a scale from 0–5, reward answers which include the following:
a) Suitable past narrative tense(s)
b) Informal register
c) Relevant vocabulary at this level
d) Generally accurate spelling
e) Use of linking language

Total mark out of 10

Listening

Part 1 Questions 1–7

1 B   2 C   3 B   4 A   5 D   6 D   7 A

Part 2 Questions 8–13

8 B   9 A   10 C   11 D   12 C   13 D

Part 3 Questions 14–19

14 family life   15 Silver Sands   16 (a) camera   17 31 August
18 over 18   19 25 East Hill

Part 4 Questions 20–25

20 B   21 A   22 B   23 B   24 A   25 A

Test 1 tapescript

This is PET Practice Test 1. There are four parts to the test. You will hear each recording twice. During the test there will be a pause before each part to allow you to look through the questions, and other pauses to let you think about your answers. You should write your answers on the question paper. You will have twelve minutes at the end to transfer your answers to the separate answer sheet.

PART 1   *Part 1. There are seven questions in this part. For each question there are four pictures and a short recording. You will hear each recording twice. For each question, look at the pictures and listen to the recording. Choose the correct picture and put a tick in the box below it.*

Before we start, here is an example:

What should the class do?

Woman: Now, to start our next exercise, I'd like you to bend over and hold your ankles with your hands.

[pause]

The woman told the class what to do. The first picture is correct, and the tick has been put in the box under the picture.

Now we are ready to start. Here is a short recording for the first four pictures. Don't forget to put a tick in one of the boxes. Listen carefully.

One. What is Tim doing at the moment?

Woman: Did Tim get that job at the bank that he wanted?
Man: He's changed his plans, actually. He's working on a farm right now but he's hoping to go to college next year to do a computer course.

[pause]

[The recording is repeated.]

[pause]

Two. Which is Peter's family?

Girl: Was that your little sister I saw you with yesterday, Peter?
Boy: No, that was my neighbour. My sisters are both older than me.

[pause]

[The recording is repeated.]

[pause]

Three. Where are the tickets?

Man: I can't find the tickets. Why have you moved them from the table?
Woman: I didn't. You left them on the shelf under the telephone.

[pause]

[The recording is repeated.]

[pause]

Four. What caused a problem?

Woman: Why are you so late? Did the roadworks hold you up again?
Girl: We didn't even see them. We had to go round the long way because the road was flooded.

[pause]

[The recording is repeated.]

[pause]

Five. What is he going to buy?

Man: I'm going out now. Shall I get some fish for dinner?
Woman: I bought some chicken and some sausages, so we don't need fish. But we're short of vegetables, so can you get some carrots, 'cause I didn't realise?

[pause]

[The recording is repeated.]

[pause]

Six. Where is the house?

Girl: I'm so pleased you're coming to see the new house. It's quite easy to find. When you get to the village, look out for the phone box on the left. Then our house is just after the crossroads at the foot of the hill.

[pause]

[The recording is repeated.]

[pause]

Seven. How did she travel?

Man: I bet you had a terrible journey. Don't you wish you'd flown after all?

Woman: Well, yes, I do, actually. In fact, we're lucky to be here! We were waiting on the wrong platform and only realised just in time. Then there was no buffet on board, and we had to stand for several hours.

[pause]

[The recording is repeated.]

[pause]

That is the end of Part 1.

You now have half a minute to check your answers. We will tell you when Part 2 begins.

[pause]

PART 2   *Now turn to Part 2, questions 8–13.*

Look at the questions for this part. You will hear a tourist guide talking about some places to visit in London. Put a tick in the correct box for each question. At the end the recording is repeated.

[pause]

Now we are ready to start. Listen carefully.

Guide: Now I'd like to tell you about one or two places you might like to go to during the week when we're not visiting anywhere as a group.

    The first is the Canal Café Theatre, which is a small sort of, well, not exactly theatre. It's quite central, the tube station is Warwick Avenue. They don't do ordinary plays, more comedy and music and things, sometimes with the audience joining in. It's usually got a good atmosphere, and they serve food as well during the performance.

    Another good place, which has been well-known for its high-quality performances is the Donmar Warehouse. This little theatre in Convent Garden also used to be famous for not being very comfortable for the audience. It's had some work done on it and is now much improved and well worth visiting.

    If you like seeing today's performers on yesterday's stage, then you should try and get to the Hackney Empire. This is a great old theatre. Inside it's just beautiful, all gold and red. It's where you can see shows by individuals well-known from television as well as groups who are popular with local audiences. You can best reach it from the British Rail station of London Fields by getting a train out from the centre.

    I also want to mention Brixton Academy, which is also a very interesting building, in Brixton, naturally, with the largest stage in Europe, where you can see some of the really great international names in rock music and dance.

    Lastly, you might consider the Drill Hall Arts Centre, where as well as food and drink they offer courses and classes, and you can watch a play or performance which will certainly be something quite new and experimental and might be from abroad. Mondays, you need to know, are for women only, which may be of interest to some of you. It's very central, near Goodge Street tube, or you can walk from this hotel.

[pause]

Now listen again.

[The recording is repeated.]

That is the end of Part 2.

You now have a minute to check your answers. We will tell you when Part 3 begins.

[pause]

PART 3   *Now turn to Part 3, questions 14–19.*

Look at the notes about a competition. Some information is missing. You will hear a radio announcer giving information about the competition. For each question, fill in the missing information in the numbered space. At the end the recording is repeated.

[pause]

Now we are ready to start. Listen carefully.

Radio announcer: And now here's news about our latest competition. You won't believe what we're offering you this month. As this is International Year of the Family, you have the chance to win a wonderful family holiday in Jamaica. All you have to do is take a photograph which shows family life. It could be children with their parents or their grandparents or whatever you wish. You don't have to have taken it on holiday of course. Now, the lucky winner has the chance to spend two weeks at Silver Sands Bay in Jamaica. Two weeks of beautiful beaches, sunshine, plenty for everyone to do. There are watersports, children's entertainments and everything is included. That's everything – food as well. Now, the second prize is a camera worth £500 and that's certainly worth having for any holidays coming up. So send us your photograph – in colour or black and white – by 31 August – that's the closing date for entries – and listen to this programme to hear if you've won or not. We will be announcing the winners on 19 September. Now, you must be over 18 years of age. I'm sorry kids, but you'll have a chance next month in our super sports competition! Send your lucky photograph to us at DCM Radio, 25 East Hill, Brighton, Sussex. And don't forget to write your name and address on the back of the photo. We can't return any photos, I'm afraid, so make sure that you've got another copy if it's your favourite.

[pause]

Now listen again.

[The recording is repeated.]

That is the end of Part 3.

You now have a minute to check your answers. We will tell you when Part 4 begins.

[pause]

PART 4   *Now turn to Part 4, questions 20–25.*

Look at the six statements for this part. You will hear a conversation between a girl, Fiona, and a boy, Robert. Decide if you think each statement is correct or incorrect. If you think it is correct, put a tick in the box under A for YES. If you think it is not correct, put a tick in the box under B for NO. At the end the recording is repeated.

[pause]

Now we are ready to start. Listen carefully.

Fiona: You look very happy, Robert. You must be pleased about something.
Robert: I am. You know how I've always wanted to go to the States? Well, I've got a job there for the summer.
Fiona: Oh, well done. I've been trying to get a job for the summer holiday too. Last year I worked in my dad's office but I didn't enjoy it very much. I'd prefer an outdoor job.
Robert: Well, listen to what I'm going to do. Maybe it would suit you too. I answered an advert to work in a children's summer camp in America. I had an interview in London and I've got the job. They're sending me to a camp in the mountains near Seattle in the north-west. I just can't wait.
Fiona: It sounds great. But what are you going to be doing?
Robert: The job title is sports leader. I'll be taking the children swimming and arranging team games for them – football and things like that I expect.
Fiona: I thought you hated football – I've never seen you play.
Robert: Well, no, I don't really like it but I can easily get in some practice before I go and I can find out the rules of American football.
Fiona: What else do you think they'll ask you to do?
Robert: Oh, outdoor activities like rock-climbing and sailing on the lake.
Fiona: It doesn't sound like your kind of job at all, Robert. I just can't imagine you taking a group of children rock climbing. You can't even swim either!
Robert: Well, I'm going to learn. I've got three months.
Fiona: Did you tell them that you couldn't swim and you'd never been rock-climbing?
Robert: No, I wanted the job.
Fiona: Well, I think you should tell them the truth. Maybe they could give you a job in the office or something.
Robert: No, I'll be all right when I get there.
Fiona: Well, it would really suit me. What's the address?

[pause]

Now listen again.

[The recording is repeated.]

That is the end of Part 4. You now have twelve minutes to check and transfer your answers to the answer sheet.

Teacher, stop the tape here and time twelve minutes.

That is the end of the test.

Test 2

Reading

Part 1 Questions 1–5
1 B   2 B   3 C   4 A   5 C

Part 2 Questions 6–10
6 D   7 G   8 A   9 E   10 C

Part 3 Questions 11–20
11 A   12 B   13 B   14 B   15 A   16 A   17 B   18 B
19 A   20 A

Part 4 Questions 21–25
21 A   22 C   23 C   24 B   25 B

Part 5 Questions 26–35
26 A   27 C   28 B   29 D   30 A   31 C   32 C
33 B   34 D   35 B

Writing

Part 1 Questions 1–5
1 of the film is 'The River of Hope'.
2 has shown it.
3 likes the main star.
4 bites him on the/his nose.
5 an exciting car chase at the end (of the film).

Part 2 Questions 6–15
Appropriate answers acceptable.

Part 3 Question 16
Task
Using a scale from 0–5, reward answers which include the following:
a) Description of course activities
b) Description of free-time activities
c) Description of other people
d) Appropriate ending
e) Appropriate length

Language
Using a scale from 0–5, reward answers which include the following:
a) Suitable past tense(s)
b) Informal register
c) Relevant vocabulary at this level
d) Generally accurate spelling

e) Use of descriptive words (e.g. adjectives and adverbs)

Total mark out of 10

Listening

Part 1 Questions 1–7

1 B   2 A   3 D   4 D   5 B   6 A   7 C

Part 2 Questions 8–13

8 D   9 C   10 B   11 B   12 C   13 A

Part 3 Questions 14–19

14 Saturday   15 (high) wall(s)   16 day   17 spring   18 all day
19 (school) summer holidays

Part 4 Questions 20–25

20 B   21 B   22 A   23 B   24 A   25 B

Test 2 tapescript

This is PET Practice Test 2. There are four parts to the test. You will hear each recording twice. During the test there will be a pause before each part to allow you to look through the questions, and other pauses to let you think about your answers. You should write your answers on the question paper. You will have twelve minutes at the end to transfer your answers to the separate answer sheet.

PART 1   *Part 1. There are seven questions in this part. For each question there are four pictures and a short recording. You will hear each recording twice. For each question, look at the pictures and listen to the recording. Choose the correct picture and put a tick in the box below it.*

Before we start, here is an example:

What should the class do?

Woman: Now, to start our next exercise, I'd like you to bend over and hold your ankles with your hands.
[pause]

The woman told the class what to do. The first picture is correct, and the tick has been put in the box under the picture.

Now we are ready to start. Here is a short recording for the first four pictures. Don't forget to put a tick in one of the boxes. Listen carefully.

One. Where is the desk?

Woman: Have you got a new desk?
Man: No, I've just moved it. I was getting too hot sitting under the window, so I put it over there opposite the door. [Oh.]

[pause]

[The recording is repeated.]

[pause]

Two. What did he buy?

Woman: Did you manage to find some boots?
Man: Well, I saw some, but they looked funny with my jeans. Then I looked in another shop and I saw a nice jacket, so I bought that.

[pause]

[The recording is repeated.]

[pause]

Three. How did they travel?

Man: How did you get to the island?
Woman: We usually go by ferry, but as it was an emergency we flew.
Man: Is there an airport there?
Woman: No, but there's a helicopter which goes every morning.

[pause]

[The recording is repeated.]

[pause]

Four. What does she want to eat?

Man: What do you want in your sandwich? We've got egg, cheese, salad, whatever you want.
Girl: Sausage and tomato, please – [OK] oh, no – I had that yesterday. I'll just have egg today.

[pause]

[The recording is repeated.]

[pause]

Five. What time will they meet?

Man: What time shall we meet? Will half past twelve suit you?
Woman: Might be a bit early actually. Um, I'll be finishing about twelve, but I've got to be back by two. So I need to leave the restaurant in time. So – yes, that should be fine, in fact.

[pause]

[The recording is repeated.]

[pause]

Six. Why were they late?

Woman: Sorry we're so late. We had to stop and get the windscreen fixed. It got hit by a stone on that new road, and we had to call the garage.

[pause]

[The recording is repeated.]

[pause]

Seven. Where did they go?

Man: How did you keep the kids amused in the rain? Did you go to the museum?
Woman: They said they'd had enough history because we went round the castle
         yesterday, so we went to the modern art gallery. [Oh.] I was surprised how
         much they enjoyed it, actually.

[pause]

[The recording is repeated.]

[pause]

That is the end of Part 1.

You now have half a minute to check your answers. We will tell you when Part 2 begins.

[pause]

PART 2   *Now turn to Part 2, questions 8–13.*

*Look at the questions for this part. You will hear someone talking about a library. Put a
tick in the correct box for each question. At the end the recording is repeated.*

[pause]

Now we are ready to start. Listen carefully.

Paul: OK. Well, Monica, I'm sure you'll enjoy working here. My name's Paul and I'm
        the librarian. [Hello.] The library's closed today because we're moving things
        around but we're open again tomorrow and when the new term starts next week
        we'll be really busy. We're open from nine in the morning until eight in the
        evening but you're not expected to be here all that time. You start work at a
        quarter to nine and finish at a quarter past five, OK? [Right, right.] The evening
        staff take over then. Right.
            Now, students aren't allowed to bring large bags into the library. But staff can
        bring their bags in and leave them in the office. And there's a drawer in your desk
        which you can lock if you bring money or anything of value in to work with you.
        OK? Now you have an hour for lunch. We don't have many rules but I don't like
        staff eating in the library [No.], for obvious reasons. Of course you can have a cup
        of coffee there while you're working. If you bring sandwiches for lunch, there's a
        common room downstairs where you can eat them. [Right.] If you want to buy
        lunch, I'd recommend the canteen upstairs – it's very good value. There are cafés
        in the town centre but it's a bit of rush to get there and back in an hour and
        they're very expensive. Oh, and there's a machine just outside the library which
        sells drinks and chocolate bars, that sort of thing. [Yes.]
            Now I'll just show you round. [Right.] This is the desk where the books come
        in and go out, and you'll spend some of your time here. But you'll spend most of
        your time putting books back onto the shelves. [Right.] You'll be responsible for
        doing that so you need to know where everything is. You'll also help with
        showing people round the library and sending out letters about books that are
        overdue. You'll be surprised how many books aren't brought back on time.
            The whole of the ground floor – that's this floor – [Yes.] contains books that
        can be borrowed. The first floor contains mainly reference books which should
        not leave the library. The top floor has desks where students can work and also
        newspapers, magazines, that sort of thing. You may sometimes need to go down
        to the basement. Now that's where we keep especially valuable books. [Right.]

Now is there anything else? Oh, can I just check the form you filled in? [Yes.] I know your name and address obviously but can you give me your telephone number? [Yes.] We've got your tax number and all the other information …

[pause]

Now listen again.

[The recording is repeated.]

That is the end of Part 2.

You now have a minute to check your answers. We will tell you when Part 3 begins.

[pause]

PART 3   *Now turn to Part 3, questions 14–19.*

Look at the notes about tourist attractions in the south of England. Some information is missing. You will hear a tourist information officer talking. For each question, fill in the missing information in the numbered space. At the end the recording is repeated.

[pause]

Now we are ready to start. Listen carefully.

Tourist information officer: Probably the best known building in this particular area is Arundel Castle. It's well worth a visit to see the beautiful furniture and paintings, and you shouldn't forget it's been in the same family for nearly a thousand years. It's open from April to October, Sundays to Fridays, from eleven in the morning. The last entrance is at four, and it closes at five. You can buy home-made food in the restaurant and of course there's a souvenir shop.

    If you'd like to get a view of the castle from outside, one way is to take a boat trip on the River Arun for the afternoon. You'll get a quite different look at the historic town of Arundel, with its old port, and you pass close under the high walls of the castle before following the Arun through typical English countryside of hills, woods and small villages. Daily trips in summer depart from Littlehampton and Arundel. The Arundel Wildfowl and Wetlands Centre is also a good place to enjoy natural beauty, with its fascinating population of water birds including ducks, geese and swans – many of them are so tame that they'll feed from your hand. It's especially interesting to visit in the spring, to see the young birds, but it's open all the year round with a gift shop and restaurant open all day, serving lunches from twelve to two.

    And lastly, what about a visit to the past at Amberley Museum? A fascinating reminder of everyday life in the early part of this century, and very educational for younger visitors. There's masses to see, so allow at least three hours. The museum is normally open from Wednesdays to Sundays, and every day throughout the long school summer holidays. And it's easy to reach too, because it's right next door to the railway station.

[pause]

Now listen again.

[The recording is repeated.]

That is the end of Part 3.

You now have a minute to check your answers. We will tell you when Part 4 begins.

[pause]

PART 4   *Now turn to Part 4, questions 20–25.*

Look at the six statements for this part. You will hear a conversation between a teenager called Thomas, and his father. Decide if you think each statement is correct or incorrect. If you think it is correct, put a tick in the box under A for YES. If you think it is not correct, put a tick in the box under B for NO. At the end the recording is repeated.

[pause]

Now we are ready to start. Listen carefully.

Thomas:	I got into the team, Dad.
Father:	That's great, Tom. I knew you could if you really went for it. So, I promised you an evening out if you made it. What do you want to do?
Thomas:	Oh, I guess we could, well, er, what about if …
Father:	Don't you want to celebrate? What about a meal? There's a Chinese restaurant just opened. It's supposed to be very good.
Thomas:	Oh, is it? Well, it's very nice of you.
Father:	Or would you rather see a film? I haven't been to the cinema for ages. What do you say?
Thomas:	Well, it's a bit late for this evening, isn't it? I mean, we'd hardly get there before it started, there aren't so many buses in the evening.
Father:	We can take the car. I don't think there'll be any problem parking at this time of day.
Thomas:	What do you want to see?
Father:	No, no, you choose. It's your evening. What about that new comedy thriller? Is that on?
Thomas:	Yes, it is, but you don't like them much, do you?
Father:	Well, no, but if that's what you'd like, let's go. It's your evening.
Thomas:	Yeah, look Dad, it's really nice of you, but I know you'll be bored. You don't have to come.
Father:	Hey, Tom, don't worry. Oh, wait a minute. What about going out tomorrow?
Thomas:	Yeah, that'd be fine.
Father:	I'm sorry. I suppose you've got something planned with the team tonight, haven't you?
Thomas:	Yeah, well, some of the boys are meeting at the burger bar.
Father:	It's OK, Tom.
Thomas:	I don't want to hurt your feelings. I mean it's really nice of you. And I do like Chinese food.
Father:	Don't give it another thought. Tomorrow's perfectly OK with me. You should have said. We'll make it tomorrow, all right?
Thomas:	Yeah. Great. Thanks, Dad. I'll be off then.
Father:	Sure. Enjoy yourself.

[pause]

Now listen again.

[The recording is repeated.]

That is the end of Part 4. You now have twelve minutes to check and transfer your answers to the answer sheet.

Teacher: stop the tape here and time twelve minutes.

That is the end of the test.

Test 3

Reading

Part 1   Questions 1–5

1 D   2 D   3 A   4 A   5 B

Part 2   Questions 6–10

6 C   7 B   8 D   9 H   10 G

Part 3   Questions 11–20

11 B   12 A   13 A   14 B   15 A   16 B   17 B   18 A
19 A   20 A

Part 4   Questions 21–25

21 C   22 C   23 B   24 A   25 B

Part 5   Questions 26–35

26 C   27 A   28 C   29 B   30 B   31 A   32 D
33 C   34 D   35 C

Writing

Part 1   Questions 1–5

1 are more expensive than / aren't so cheap as the airport bus.
2 are sold / are for sale in the departure lounge.
3 has a post office.
4 owns the Hotel Atlanta.
5 likes the Happy Traveller Café.

Part 2   Questions 6–15

Appropriate answers acceptable.

Part 3   Question 16

Task
Using a scale from 0–5, reward answers which include the following:
a) Directions for reaching college
b) Mention of the possibility of their arriving before classes end
c) Description of thing(s) to do near college
d) Appropriate ending
e) Appropriate length

Language
Using a scale from 0–5, reward answers which include the following:
a) Suitable imperative and/or other tense(s)
b) Informal register
c) Relevant vocabulary at this level
d) Generally accurate spelling

e) Use of conditional or other appropriate tense for talking about arrival time, e.g. 'If you arrive early, you can ... '

Total mark out of 10

Listening

Part 1 Questions 1–7

1 D   2 A   3 A   4 C   5 B   6 D   7 C

Part 2 Questions 8–13

8 A   9 D   10 B   11 C   12 B   13 D

Part 3 Questions 14–19

14 seven / 7 (o'clock)   15 nine-thirty / 9.30   16 college porter
17 health check   18 shows   19 low-price / cheap

Part 4 Questions 20–25

20 A   21 B   22 A   23 B   24 A   25 B

Test 3 tapescript

This is PET Practice Test 3. There are four parts to the test. You will hear each recording twice. During the test there will be a pause before each part to allow you to look through the questions, and other pauses to let you think about your answers. You should write your answers on the question paper. You will have twelve minutes at the end to transfer your answers to the separate answer sheet.

PART 1   *Part 1. There are seven questions in this part. For each question there are four pictures and a short recording. You will hear each recording twice. For each question, look at the pictures and listen to the recording. Choose the correct picture and put a tick in the box below it.*

Before we start, here is an example:

What should the class do?

Woman: Now, to start our next exercise, I'd like you to bend over and hold your ankles with your hands.

[pause]

The woman told the class what to do. The first picture is correct, and the tick has been put in the box under the picture.

Now we are ready to start. Here is a short recording for the first four pictures. Don't forget to put a tick in one of the boxes. Listen carefully.

One. What are they going to buy?

Woman: We need to get something for Jim. It's his last day at work tomorrow.
Man: Um, he's a quiet person. Um, what about a cassette or a book?
Woman: But we don't know what he likes. Something to wear? Gloves? Or, I tell you what, a tie. Then it doesn't matter about the size.
Man: OK.

[pause]

[The recording is repeated.]

[pause]

Two. Where is the butter?

Girl: Can you get some butter out of the fridge?
Boy: I can't see it.
Girl: It's at the top above those bottles of juice.
Boy: Oh, yes. I've got it.

[pause]

[The recording is repeated.]

[pause]

Three. What does he want to buy?

Man: Can I have two of those postcards of the castle, please?
Woman: Do you want the big ones or the small ones?
Man: One of each, please.

[pause]

[The recording is repeated.]

[pause]

Four. What is he washing?

Man: Can you turn the radio on for me? I want to listen to it while I finish this washing-up.

[pause]

[The recording is repeated.]

[pause]

Five. Where must he go?

Man: Can you tell me where the head teacher's office is, please?
Boy: Go to the end of this corridor, turn left, and it's the door facing you.

[pause]

[The recording is repeated.]

[pause]

Six. What's in the photograph?

Girl: We really enjoyed going to the wildlife park. There were lions and tigers, and here's a photograph I took of the camels. We liked the baby elephants best but I didn't manage to get a picture of them.

[pause]

[The recording is repeated.]

[pause]

Seven. What has he hurt?

Man: What's wrong with your foot?
Boy: It's not that. It's my knee – I hurt it playing hockey the other day.

[pause]

[The recording is repeated.]

[pause]

That is the end of Part 1.

You now have half a minute to check your answers. We will tell you when Part 2 begins.

[pause]

PART 2   *Now turn to Part 2, questions 8–13.*

Look at the questions for this part. You will hear part of a radio travel programme. Put a tick in the correct box for each question. At the end the recording is repeated.

[pause]

Now we are ready to start. Listen carefully.

Presenter: In our series 'Seeing Europe' today we look at ideas for seeing England without a car. And I've tried them all myself.
First I went on a cycling holiday with a tour company. They provide accommodation, bikes and a van to carry luggage, so you can enjoy the countryside. Our group included teenagers, who got a lot of fun racing each other. You don't need to be superfit; in fact, I'd say we were too slow for experienced cyclists. The price covers everything except lunches. We stayed in small hotels, or farms offering bed and breakfast, which were very comfortable. My only complaint was that the restaurants where we stopped for lunch were rather expensive. If you wanted to save money, you'd have to buy food during the morning and picnic in a field while the others were having their lunch. Generally, though, well worth considering.
Next I tried a canal boat with some friends. This is another way to see beautiful countryside and escape the traffic. Hiring a boat is not cheap. It costs as much as some foreign holidays, but ours was very comfortable. The price included everything except food, and by the end, we felt we really hadn't spent too much, we'd had such a good time. I was a bit nervous about managing the boat, as none of us had done it before, but you get plenty of advice. You meet all sorts of people, but they all enjoy a chat. As one old man said to me, 'We all get wet some time!' And they'll explain what to do, and by the end of the week you can laugh at your early mistakes.
Lastly, I toured around, using tourist offices to book accommodation with a local family each day. You have to choose towns with tourist offices of course, and I soon learnt to go straight there when I arrived, because this service only runs till four in the afternoon. The tourist office makes the booking over the phone for you and you pay the landlady before you leave. I travelled by bus, as it's cheaper, and the bus station is usually in the town centre, unlike the railway station, if there is one. For very long journeys, trains are more comfortable, although travelling from east to west you often

have to go into London and out again, which is a waste of time. All in all, on these trips I felt I was seeing the real England.

[pause]

Now listen again.

[The recording is repeated.]

That is the end of Part 2.

You now have a minute to check your answers. We will tell you when Part 3 begins.

[pause]

PART 3   *Now turn to Part 3, questions 14–19.*

Look at the notes. Some information is missing. You will hear someone talking about the sports and social club at her place of work. For each question, fill in the missing information in the numbered space. At the end the recording is repeated.

[pause]

Now we are ready to start. Listen carefully.

Young secretary: Well, I've been asked to give you some information about what's available here for sports and other free-time activities. Right. Well, we're very lucky because we can use the swimming pool at the college next door. It opens at seven in the mornings, and we can use it before work, and also in the evenings between six and seven. It's reserved for the college between nine and six in the day and from seven till nine-thirty in the evenings. We can use it after that, and it's open till ten-thirty, but most people who work here don't want to come back into town that late. There are also two tennis courts, which we can book through the college porter.

In this building, there's a fitness centre, with all the usual sorts of equipment. That's not usually busy except at lunchtimes. If you haven't used that sort of thing before, you should sign up on the notice board outside the dining-room – that's for a health check – and then they'll show you how to use the equipment so you don't injure yourself.

We have quite a lot of clubs and groups here. For example there's the jazz dance society. They meet every Wednesday at six. Beginners are very welcome, but you have to learn quickly and be prepared to take part in shows and so on from time to time. There's also a music society. This is so that we can offer tickets for concerts at special low prices. We go to concerts about twice a month. Usually classical, but sometimes folk or rock, if there's something a lot of people are interested in.

Apart from that, there's the Entertainment Committee. There are more details about what they do on the notice board. Well, I think that's it.

[pause]

Now listen again.

[The recording is repeated.]

That is the end of Part 3.

You now have a minute to check your answers. We will tell you when Part 4 begins.

[pause]

PART 4   *Now turn to Part 4, questions 20–25.*

Look at the six statements for this part. You will hear a conversation between Wendy, who runs a clothes shop, and Mike, one of her assistants. Decide if you think each statement is correct or incorrect. If you think it is correct, put a tick in the box under A for YES. If you think it is not correct, put a tick in the box under B for NO. At the end the recording is repeated.

[pause]

Now we are ready to start. Listen carefully.

Wendy: Could we just have a quick word, please Mike?
Mike: Of course. Is anything wrong?
Wendy: Well, I hope not. It's just that I could hear what you were saying to that woman who you were serving this morning and I wondered, well, if you realised that, er, she thought you weren't being very polite.
Mike: Me? It was her that was being rude.
Wendy: In what way?
Mike: She didn't like any of the things I showed her. She picked them up and dropped them all over the place. One of the silk shirts nearly fell on the floor.
Wendy: The customers have to look at things before they buy them.
Mike: But it took me ages to put them all back in their packets.
Wendy: Well, isn't that partly what you're here for?
Mike: I suppose so. But I still think she could consider how much work she's making. People like her wouldn't be so bad if they were spending a lot of money. But in the end she just left and said she might be back later.
Wendy: And she probably will be. She's a regular customer. But she won't bother if you make her feel she's a nuisance. She'll go somewhere where the assistants seem pleased to take trouble for her, even on the days when she doesn't buy anything in the end.
Mike: OK. I get the message.
Wendy: Good. And don't forget, your job is to help the customers, not just to sell things. After all, I don't count your sales before I decide how much to pay you each week, do I?
Mike: No, I see what you mean.
Man: Excuse me.
Mike: Good afternoon sir, can I help you?
Man: Well, I'm looking for a jacket, something suitable …

[pause]

Now listen again.

[The recording is repeated.]

That is the end of Part 4. You now have twelve minutes to check and transfer your answers to the answer sheet.

Teacher: stop the tape here and time twelve minutes.

That is the end of the test.

Test 4

Reading

Part 1 Questions 1–5

1 A   2 C   3 D   4 A   5 C

Part 2 Questions 6–10

6 C   7 G   8 E   9 B   10 D

Part 3 Questions 11–20

11 A   12 B   13 A   14 B   15 A   16 B   17 B   18 B
19 A   20 B

Part 4 Questions 21–25

21 D   22 A   23 C   24 B   25 C

Part 5 Questions 26–35

26 B   27 C   28 A   29 B   30 D   31 A   32 B
33 B   34 C   35 A

Writing

Part 1 Questions 1–5

1 busy to see you now.
2 smaller than the new one / not as/so big as the new one.
3 see the doctor / go to the doctor's on Sundays / a Sunday.
4 necessary/needed on Saturdays.
5 should be taken after meals.

Part 2 Questions 6–15

Appropriate answers acceptable.

Part 3 Question 16

Task
Using a scale from 0–5, reward answers which include the following:
a) Relevant information about self
b) Description of level of English
c) Reference to personal qualities
d) Appropriate ending
e) Appropriate length

Language
Using a scale from 0–5, reward answers which include the following:
a) Suitable present etc. tense(s)
b) Formal/neutral register
c) Relevant vocabulary at this level
d) Generally accurate spelling

e) Clear organisation

Total mark out of 10

Listening

Part 1   Questions 1–7

1 A   2 A   3 C   4 D   5 D   6 B   7 A

Part 2   Questions 8–13

8 C   9 A   10 B   11 D   12 A   13 C

Part 3   Questions 14–19

14 Newtown   15 bus   16 walk   17 tent   18 (small) saucepan
19 3.45 / a quarter to four

Part 4   Questions 20–25

20 A   21 B   22 B   23 A   24 A   25 B

Test 4 tapescript

This is PET Practice Test 4. There are four parts to the test. You will hear each recording twice. During the test there will be a pause before each part to allow you to look through the questions, and other pauses to let you think about your answers. You should write your answers on the question paper. You will have twelve minutes at the end to transfer your answers to the separate answer sheet.

PART 1   *Part 1. There are seven questions in this part. For each question there are four pictures and a short recording. You will hear each recording twice. For each question, look at the pictures and listen to the recording. Choose the correct picture and put a tick in the box below it.*

Before we start, here is an example:

What should the class do?

Woman: Now, to start our next exercise, I'd like you to bend over and hold your ankles with your hands.

[pause]

The woman told the class what to do. The first picture is correct, and the tick has been put in the box under the picture.

Now we are ready to start. Here is a short recording for the first four pictures. Don't forget to put a tick in one of the boxes. Listen carefully.

One. Which mug did he get?

Woman: Did your brother give you a birthday present in the end?
Boy: Yes, a really horrible mug. It's got little flowers all over it.
Woman: What a pity, there're such nice ones around now.

[pause]

[The recording is repeated.]

Key

[pause]

Two. What has arrived?

Man: Has the post come? There should be a letter for me from the bank.
Woman: There's a postcard and a small parcel, but there aren't any letters at all, I'm
             afraid.

[pause]

[The recording is repeated.]

[pause]

Three. Which sport is she training for?

Girl: I'm training every day at the moment. I really want to get into the school hockey
         team. I've even given up playing tennis on Saturdays.

[pause]

[The recording is repeated.]

[pause]

Four. How will she travel?

Woman: I'll be back late this evening. John can't take me to the bus station in his car, so
             I'll walk down and get a later one than usual.

[pause]

[The recording is repeated.]

[pause]

Five. What does he want to buy?

Man 1: Have you got everything you need for the new flat?
Man 2: Well, I've got most things – I've got a bed and a sofa, but I'd like to get a really
            comfortable chair to go with my desk.

[pause]

[The recording is repeated.]

[pause]

Six. Which door can she use?

Girl 1: If I'm not home by the time you get there, you can let yourself into the garden
            with this key. It opens the door in the fence at the side of the house.
Girl 2: OK, thanks.

[pause]

[The recording is repeated.]

[pause]

Seven. What has she been doing?

Man: Aren't you coming to the cookery class this term?

Woman: I'd like to come again but I'm spending all my time painting the outside of the house. I have to get it done before the winter. I haven't even had time to do any gardening.

[pause]

[The recording is repeated.]

That is the end of Part 1.

You now have half a minute to check your answers. We will tell you when Part 2 begins.

[pause]

PART 2   *Now turn to Part 2, questions 8–13.*

Look at the questions for this part. You will hear some travel news on the radio. Put a tick in the correct box for each question. At the end the recording is repeated.

[pause]

Now we are ready to start. Listen carefully.

Announcer: And after that, we have a round-up of the latest information for the region's travellers. First of all, I have to warn drivers that there are delays on both roads leading into the city centre from the motorway.

Next, I must remind you that the bridge in Appletree Avenue is still closed, as it was yesterday, while last week's flood damage is being repaired. We've heard that the engineers are still not sure how long it will take to make the bridge safe again for vehicles to use.

And one last point for drivers: repair work means that the part of London Road which is north of the High Street is still only open to vehicles travelling northwards. But I understand it should be open to traffic in both directions before this evening's rush hour. So that's one piece of good news.

Now, for those of you on foot, it's worth avoiding River Street because the pavement there is temporarily out of use. The wall of the school playground has fallen down right across the pavement. Not very good news for the pupils and staff either. Bad luck – we hope the builders fix it quickly!

Well, that's all the travel news as such, but one item which might be of interest is that the Minister of Transport is visiting the city tomorrow to meet the mayor and other local government officials before opening the new technology college. He'll be walking around the city centre for about half an hour before his meeting, and the notice I have here says he's keen to hear what local people think about plans for new roads in the area.

So this is your chance if you've got strong feelings!

And the region's weather for today: starting with a few foggy patches, which will soon clear to give a mostly fine day, but we are warned that it may get a bit cold in the evening and that this will last for the next few days.

That's all for now. The next travel news will be in one hour's time after the eight o'clock news, at eight ten. Till then, over to Julia and some more morning music.

[pause]

Now listen again.

[The recording is repeated.]

That is the end of Part 2.

You now have a minute to check your answers. We will tell you when Part 3 begins.

[pause]

PART 3   *Now turn to Part 3, questions 14–19.*

Look at Polly's notes about a camping trip with her friend Sue. Some information is missing. You will hear Sue talking to Polly. For each question, fill in the missing information in the numbered space. At the end the recording is repeated.

[pause]

Now we are ready to start. Listen carefully.

Sue: Hi, Polly. This is Sue. I was just ringing to check you can still come camping at the weekend. Oh you can, good! Well, Friday afternoon to Monday morning? Great, that gives us a nice long weekend. Well, I thought it was probably better not to go too far because the weather hasn't been too good this week and if it rains all the time we might want to come home. So how about going to Newtown, which is about three miles over the border into Wales? There's a campsite just outside the town so we can catch a bus into Newtown and then walk to the campsite, which is on a farm. Yes, well I stayed there once about five years ago with my parents. We had a car but it's not far from the town. It's a beautiful spot. What do you think? Oh good. Well, the next thing is what will we need to take? You've got a tent, haven't you? So you can bring that? It's not too heavy is it? Oh good, one of those lightweight ones, I know. There's no need to bring much food because you can eat at the farmhouse – they do wonderful evening meals but we'll need a saucepan for boiling water for drinks. I can bring something to cook on but have you got a small saucepan? Good, can you bring that then? And we'll buy coffee and milk in the town when we get there. We want to get there in good time on Friday so shall I meet you in the bus station at quarter to four on Friday? OK. I'll check the bus times but I think the buses are on the hour so there should be one at four o'clock. We'll be there by five then. And I'll ring the farmer to say we're coming. OK then. Yes, I know, I'm really looking forward to it too. See you on Friday then. Bye.

[pause]

Now listen again.

[The recording is repeated.]

That is the end of Part 3.

You now have a minute to check your answers. We will tell you when Part 4 begins.

[pause]

PART 4   *Now turn to Part 4, questions 20–25.*

Look at the six statements for this part. You will hear a conversation between a man, David, and a woman, Anne, who have just returned from holiday. Decide if you think each statement is correct or incorrect. If you think it is correct, put a tick in the box under A for YES. *If you think it is not correct, put a tick in the box under B for NO. At the end the recording is repeated.*

[pause]

Now we are ready to start. Listen carefully.

David: Oh, I am glad to be home after that long flight.

Anne: Well that fog did make it longer than we expected. Let's have something to eat and drink before we unpack.

David: OK, I'll go and see if there's any food in the kitchen. Well, there's no bread – and a little bit of milk – pooh – but it smells a bit so I don't think we should use it. Is black coffee all right?

Anne: Yes, that's fine. I need more than a sandwich anyway. I'm really hungry. Have a look and see what's in the freezer.

David: OK, we could have some fish maybe. Well, that's strange. Come here, Anne.

Anne: What is it?

David: Well, the freezer's almost empty. Did we leave it like this?

Anne: Er, no. There was quite a lot of food in there. That's odd.

David: Richard must have eaten it. We let him stay in our flat while we're on holiday and he eats all our food. It's too bad.

Anne: Well, I expect he's going to pay us for it.

David: That doesn't help us now, does it, when we haven't got anything to eat.

Anne: No. Well, maybe he's at the supermarket right now buying us some food.

David: It is 10.30 at night you know. The supermarkets round here aren't open.

Anne: Oh yes. I'm a bit confused after that long flight. I'm sure there's a simple explanation – Richard's a good friend. He wouldn't cheat us.

David: He was a good friend, you mean. We said he could stay here, and he eats all our food and he hasn't cleaned up either. Look, the kitchen's really dirty.

Anne: Let's talk about it tomorrow. We can phone him and talk to him.

David: You'd better talk to him. I'm too angry.

Anne: OK. Now, let's go out and see if we can get anything to eat.

[pause]

Now listen again.

[The recording is repeated.]

That is the end of Part 4. You now have twelve minutes to check and transfer your answers to the answer sheet.

Teacher: *stop the tape here and time twelve minutes.*

That is the end of the test.

Test 5

Reading

Part 1 Questions 1–5

1 B   2 C   3 D   4 B   5 B

Part 2 Questions 6–10

6 H   7 E   8 D   9 F   10 G

Part 3 Questions 11–20

11 B   12 B   13 A   14 B   15 A   16 A   17 A
18 A   19 B   20 B

Part 4 Questions 21–25

21 C   22 B   23 D   24 B   25 A

Part 5 Questions 26–35

26 B   27 C   28 D   29 A   30 B   31 C   32 D
33 A   34 B   35 C

Writing

Part 1 Questions 1–5

1 must/have/'ve got to return the book on Monday (Danny)'.
2 has (got) / contains 80,000 books.
3 borrow books (from the library).
4 is less helpful than / not as/so helpful as the science librarian.
5 pay (a charge of) £2.

Part 2 Questions 6–15

Appropriate answers acceptable.

Part 3 Question 16

Task
Using a scale from 0–5, reward answers which include the following:
a) Description of place
b) Description of own reactions
c) Expressing links between a) and b)
d) Appropriate ending
e) Appropriate length

Language
Using a scale from 0–5, reward answers which include the following:
a) Suitable past narrative tense(s)
b) Informal register
c) Relevant vocabulary at this level
d) Generally accurate spelling

e) Use of linking language

Total mark out of 10

Listening

Part 1 Questions 1–7

1 C   2 B   3 C   4 D   5 D   6 A   7 A

Part 2 Questions 8–13

8 C   9 B   10 A   11 A   12 C   13 C

Part 3 Questions 14–19

14 Italy   15 rich   16 Germany   17 women's / woman's
18 soldiers   19 feelings

Part 4 Questions 20–25

20 A   21 B   22 B   23 B   24 A   25 A

Test 5 tapescript

This is PET Practice Test 5. There are four parts to the test. You will hear each recording twice. During the test there will be a pause before each part to allow you to look through the questions, and other pauses to let you think about your answers. You should write your answers on the question paper. You will have twelve minutes at the end to transfer your answers to the separate answer sheet.

PART 1   *Part 1. There are seven questions in this part. For each question there are four pictures and a short recording. You will hear each recording twice. For each question, look at the pictures and listen to the recording. Choose the correct picture and put a tick in the box below it.*

Before we start, here is an example:

What should the class do?

Woman: Now, to start our next exercise, I'd like you to bend over and hold your ankles with your hands.

[pause]

The woman told the class what to do. The first picture is correct, and the tick has been put in the box under the picture.

Now we are ready to start. Here is a short recording for the first four pictures. Don't forget to put a tick in one of the boxes. Listen carefully.

One. What is wrong with her?

Woman: I've got a really sore throat, doctor.
Doctor: Oh, yes. Do you have a headache or a stomachache as well?
Woman: No, neither.
Doctor: Let's just have a look then.

[pause]

[The recording is repeated.]

[pause]

Two. What's Alice going to do this afternoon?

Girl: Is Alice coming to the cinema with us this afternoon?
Boy: I don't think so. She's been so busy studying for her exams, she said she's got to do some shopping before she runs out of food completely!

[pause]

[The recording is repeated.]

[pause]

Three. What was the weather like?

Woman: I suppose you had all sorts of weather when you were in the States?
Man: Well, of course, where I was it was very sunny and hot, although I didn't notice most of the time. Everywhere has air-conditioning, in fact a lot of the buildings are almost too cold.

[pause]

[The recording is repeated.]

[pause]

Four. Where is he putting the television?

Man: Why don't we move the television on top of this cupboard? Then we can hide the wires behind it.

[pause]

[The recording is repeated.]

[pause]

Five. Which sport does she do now?

Man: You're looking very fit. Have you started jogging or something?
Woman: I did it for a while but I find running so boring. I've been going swimming recently instead.
Man: Well, it's certainly done you a lot of good.

[pause]

[The recording is repeated.]

[pause]

Six. Which is the manager?

Boy: How will I know which one's the manager?
Girl: He's fairly tall, um, not much hair, and he usually looks rather cross.

[pause]

[The recording is repeated.]

[pause]

Seven. Which is the house?

Woman: When I got there I couldn't find their house. I usually know it by the tree in the front garden, but they've cut it down. And they've changed the curtains. They've got plain ones now instead of the patterned ones they've always had.

[pause]

[The recording is repeated.]

[pause]

That is the end of Part 1.

You now have half a minute to check your answers. We will tell you when Part 2 begins.

[pause]

PART 2   *Now turn to Part 2, questions 8–13.*

Look at the questions for this part. You will hear someone talking about jobs for young people in Australia. Put a tick in the correct box for each question. At the end the recording is repeated.

[pause]

Now we are ready to start. Listen carefully.

Man: You're getting a lot of information today about how to get jobs abroad for those of you who are tired of being in Britain and want to travel and work at the same time. You've heard about Europe. Now I'm going to tell you about Australia. There's a huge amount to say as Australia is a huge country. People go there for a few weeks and expect to be able to see everything. If you go there to work, try to allow at least two months for travelling at the end of your stay.

There's a very useful organisation called BUNAC – that's B-U-N-A-C. OK, got that? BUNAC's aim is to help young people who want to spend some time in Australia. It's open to anybody from the United Kingdom, Ireland, the Netherlands or Canada and you have to be aged between 18 and 30. The only other thing they require is that you have £1000 left in the bank after you've paid for your flight. Yeah? They'll help you to find a job, arrange health and other insurance, they'll book flights for you and arrange accommodation for the first two nights after you arrive but after that you have to find your own accommodation.

Another useful organisation is the Australian Trust for the Environment. If you're over 17 and are fit and well, they can help you find a job on a farm, in the countryside or helping in schools. But you do need to be able to understand and speak good English though. You won't earn much, but they can find you a job for up to six months if you want to stay that long.

Seasonal work can be found through Templines. They can find you a job for one or two months at a time. They always have jobs available picking tobacco in Northern Queensland in late September and in central Victoria in late January.

On that subject, Australia grows a lot of fruit from apples to pineapples and bananas and of course grapes, which supply the increasingly successful wine industry. It's difficult to arrange these jobs from Britain but if you're in Australia in February or March, you're sure to find some work picking grapes.

I've run out of time unfortunately, so if you want some more information, I suggest you take one of our booklets. That contains all the details I've given you as well as useful phone numbers and addresses.

[pause]

Now listen again.

[The recording is repeated.]

That is the end of Part 2.

You now have a minute to check your answers. We will tell you when Part 3 begins.

[pause]

PART 3   *Now turn to Part 3, questions 14–19.*

Look at the notes. Some information is missing. You will hear a student talking to her class about a famous person. For each question, fill in the missing information in the numbered space. At the end the recording is repeated.

[pause]

Now we are ready to start. Listen carefully.

Student: I want to talk about a very special woman, a woman who was responsible for saving many, many lives and who had a great influence on the way we are treated when we are ill. Her name is Florence Nightingale. She was born in 1820. Her family, um, her family, were English, but she wasn't born in England, but in Italy. Her parents were the sort of rich people who could afford to go on long foreign tours, and this was where they happened to be when she was born. Anyway, she grew up in England and she enjoyed the typical life of a young lady of her class at that time. But she was quite a serious young person and she gradually realised that she wanted more in life than elegant clothes and a rich husband. And, um, when she was twenty-five, she said that, she announced that she wished to become a nurse and she left her comfortable home in England and she went to Germany, where they had modern training courses for nurses. Um, in 1853 she was put in charge of a women's hospital in London and she ran it very successfully. A few years later there was hardly anybody, there was hardly anyone in England who didn't know Florence Nightingale. And this was because she went abroad to care for soldiers who had been wounded fighting for their country. And she was really shocked, she was really angry when she found out how bad the army hospital was and she persuaded the government back in London to introduce many improvements. She was very popular with her patients and she continued to work for many more years, training and organising. Um, she insisted on things that we still believe nowadays. For example, nurses should always be neat and clean. And she never let them forget that patients have feelings which nurses must consider when they're looking after them.

[pause]

Now listen again.

[The recording is repeated.]

That is the end of Part 3.

You now have a minute to check your answers. We will tell you when Part 4 begins.

[pause]

PART 4   *Now turn to Part 4, questions 20–25.*

Look at the six statements for this part. You will hear a conversation between a boy, John, and a girl, Katie. Decide if you think each statement is correct or incorrect. If you think it is correct, put a tick in the box under A for YES. If you think it is not correct, put a tick in the box under B for NO. At the end the recording is repeated.

[pause]

Now we are ready to start. Listen carefully.

John: Did you have a nice weekend?
Katie: Well, I didn't actually. You know my Italian flatmate Anna?
John: I thought she was English.
Katie: Well, she speaks perfect English because she's lived here since she was 15. Well, some Italian friends came to visit her and they spent the whole weekend speaking Italian, laughing and joking together. And I couldn't understand a word. They can speak English but they refuse to speak it together.
John: Well, it must be very difficult for them to speak English to each other when they're all Italian. Didn't they try to speak English to you?
Katie: Well, they talked to me in English a bit but only to say things like 'Do you want a coffee?' As soon as they wanted to say something interesting they changed to Italian.
John: Maybe their English isn't good enough to say everything they wanted.
Katie: Well, I think they should make an effort when they're in England.
John: That's silly. Would you speak Italian to me if we were in Italy? Course you wouldn't. It's much easier to speak English. You need to think of their point of view.
Katie: The worst thing was that when I complained about it to Anna we had a big argument. She said she hardly ever has the chance to speak Italian and she was really enjoying herself.
John: Well, I can understand that. She needs to be able to speak Italian sometimes. Didn't she tell you these friends were coming?
Katie: Yes, she did but she didn't tell me they were going to speak Italian all the time.
John: Next time they come, why don't you arrange to do something else? Then Anna can enjoy their company without having to worry about you. Or you could learn some Italian.
Katie: Anna did offer to teach me.
John: Well, why don't you take it up? You could get to know her friends then.
Katie: Yes, I think I will. They seem to be really nice people.

[pause]

Now listen again.

[The recording is repeated.]

That is the end of Part 4. You now have twelve minutes to check and transfer your answers to the answer sheet.

Teacher: stop the tape here and time twelve minutes.

That is the end of the test.

Acknowledgements

The assessment criteria on pp. 46 and 53 and the sample answer sheets in the Student's Book are reproduced by kind permission of the University of Cambridge Local Examinations Syndicate.